Alan Titchmarsh
how to garden

Weekend Gardening

Alan **Titchmarsh**
how to garden

Weekend Gardening

BOOKS

10 9 8 7 6 5 4 3 2 1

Published in 2012 by BBC Books, an imprint of
Ebury Publishing, a Random House Group Company

The Random House Group Limited Reg. No. 954009

Addresses for companies within the Random House
Group can be found at **www.randomhouse.co.uk**

The Random House Group Limited
supports the Forest Stewardship
Council® (FSC®), the leading
international forest certification
organisation. All our titles that are
printed on Greenpeace approved
FSC® certified paper carry the
FSC® logo. Our paper procurement
policy can be found at www.
rbooks.co.uk/environment

FSC
www.fsc.org
MIX
Paper from
responsible sources
FSC™ C004592

A CIP catalogue record for this book is available from
the British Library.

ISBN 978 1 84 990218 2

Produced by OutHouse!
Shalbourne, Marlborough, Wiltshire SN8 3QJ

BBC BOOKS
COMMISSIONING EDITOR: Lorna Russell
PROJECT EDITOR: Caroline McArthur
PRODUCTION: Rebecca Jones

OUTHOUSE!
COMMISSIONING EDITOR: Sue Gordon
SERIES EDITOR & PROJECT EDITOR: Polly Boyd
SERIES ART DIRECTOR: Robin Whitecross
CONTRIBUTING EDITOR: Jo Weeks
DESIGNERS: Heather McCarry, Louise Turpin
ILLUSTRATIONS by Caroline De Lane Lea, Lizzie Harper,
Susan Hillier, Janet Tanner
PHOTOGRAPHS by Jonathan Buckley except where
credited otherwise on page 96
CONCEPT DEVELOPMENT & SERIES DESIGN:
Elizabeth Mallard-Shaw, Sharon Cluett

Colour origination by Altaimage, London
Printed and bound by Firmengruppe APPL,
Wemding, Germany

Contents

Introduction

Gardening is one of the best and most fulfilling activities on earth, but it can sometimes seem complicated and confusing. The answers to problems can usually be found in books, but big fat gardening books can be rather daunting. Where do you start? How can you find just the information you want without wading through lots of stuff that is not appropriate to your particular problem? Well, a good index is helpful, but sometimes a smaller book devoted to one particular subject fits the bill better – especially if it is reasonably priced and if you have a small garden where you might not be able to fit in everything suggested in a larger volume.

The *How to Garden* books aim to fill that gap – even if sometimes it may be only a small one. They are clearly set out and written, I hope, in a straightforward, easy-to-understand style. I don't see any point in making gardening complicated, when much of it is based on common sense and observation. (All the key techniques are explained and illustrated, and I've included plenty of tips and tricks of the trade.)

There are suggestions on the best plants and the best varieties to grow in particular situations and for a particular effect. I've tried to keep the information crisp and to the point so that you can find what you need quickly and easily and then put your new-found knowledge into practice. Don't worry if you're not familiar with the Latin names of plants. They are there to make sure you can find the plant as it will be labelled in the nursery or garden centre, but where appropriate I have included common names, too. Forgetting a plant's name need not stand in your way when it comes to being able to grow it.

Above all, the *How to Garden* books are designed to fill you with passion and enthusiasm for your garden and all that its creation and care entails, from designing and planting it to maintaining it and enjoying it. For more than fifty years gardening has been my passion, and that initial enthusiasm for watching plants grow, for trying something new and for just being outside pottering has never faded. If anything I am keener on gardening now than I ever was and get more satisfaction from my plants every day. It's not that I am simply a romantic, but rather that I have learned to look for the good in gardens and in plants, and there is lots to be found. Oh, there are times when I fail – when my plants don't grow as well as they should and I need to try harder. But where would I rather be on a sunny day? Nowhere!

The *How to Garden* handbooks will, I hope, allow some of that enthusiasm – childish though it may be – to rub off on you, and the information they contain will, I hope, make you a better gardener, as well as opening your eyes to the magic of plants and flowers.

Designing for less work

Sometimes the idea of having a lovely garden can seem like an unobtainable dream, especially when you're busy working or raising a family, or as you become less energetic with the passing years. However, by doing some careful planning and choosing suitable plants, it is certainly possible to create a beautiful garden and keep it looking good in just a few hours a week.

Less work, more time

Low-maintenance gardens can have just as many plants and features as labour-intensive ones – it's simply that they're easier to care for. If you want to reduce your workload, but still have a garden to be proud of, start by identifying the key components and looking at how much maintenance is involved in each. Then you can look at ways to make changes, giving you more time to enjoy your garden in whatever way you wish.

The plants

Top of the high-maintenance list are the plants, particularly those grown for their flowers. Luckily, they are also the reason why most of us have gardens and why we enjoy them, otherwise easy-care gardens would be more or less plant-free.

Labour-saving choices

To start cutting down on the time you spend growing plants, you need to be aware of the ways in which they create work.

First, there is the process of planting, which is fun, quick and easy – hardly work at all, so long as you've prepared the site properly (*see* pages 37–8). Second, there is the maintenance. Some plants grow happily year after year without much attention, while others need feeding, pruning, dividing, tying in, dead-heading, digging up and protecting over winter and so on. Choosing plants with their maintenance requirements in mind is one of the best ways to keep your gardening time under control. The directory (*see* pages 64–91) describes many high-performance, low-maintenance

plants. It also makes good sense to choose plants that will thrive in the conditions in your garden, because then they won't constantly be fighting to survive (*see* pages 58–63 for ideas for difficult situations).

Growing plants in raised beds often makes life easier and reduces

maintenance (*see* pages 34 and 52–3). In larger gardens, there is always the option of having different levels of tidiness in your flower beds, with areas close to the house being kept neat and trim, while those further away are allowed to become less formal. Planting shrubs and trees into grass, for example, reduces weeding work. (For more on plants and plant care, *see* pages 37–43.)

The lawn

Some gardeners might argue that grass is higher maintenance than flowering plants, but that is only if you want a lawn with turf like a

A combination of raised beds and foliage plants looks good throughout the year and is very easy to care for.

bowling green. The common-or-garden lawn that does perfectly well for the vast majority of us just needs a quick mow once a week along with some more extensive work in spring and autumn. As a rule of thumb, it takes about 20 or 30 seconds to mow a square metre of lawn and about five or ten minutes to weed the same amount of flower bed.

Easy-care lawns and meadows

There are several ways to reduce the amount of time spent on the lawn. First, make it an easy shape to mow and put in a permanent mowing edge around the lawn to avoid having to cut the edges. Also, you can allow the grass to grow a little longer between mowings. Again, areas near the house could be kept neater and those further away allowed to grow longer. (For more on creating and maintaining a lawn, *see* pages 22–4.)

Meadow areas of quite long grass, perhaps interspersed with wildflowers and paths mown through it, look lovely and are also very popular with wildlife. They're not completely maintenance-free and need careful preparatory work, but in the end they require less regular care than a lawn. A wildflower meadow filled with flowering bulbs in spring and poppies and cornflowers in summer can be just as decorative as a flower bed. (For how to make a wildflower mini-meadow, *see* pages 48–9.)

The hard surfaces

So long as they're properly laid, hard surfaces, such as patios, paths and steps, are all fairly easy to look after. A garden consisting entirely of hard surfaces and no grass would be very low maintenance, but bear in mind a combination of surfaces is often more interesting than simply using one material throughout (*see* left).

Paving slabs, bricks and concrete are the easiest to care for: a sweep over every month will keep them in good shape, plus a once- or twice-yearly pressure-wash, especially on shady areas, where algae is more likely to grow. Good-quality decking is also fairly easy to look after, as long as it's in a sunny area, but give it a good clean and restain annually.

Gravel and bark are both useful for paths and informal seating areas. They can be more work than solid surfaces, as they need regular weeding and picking over to remove fallen leaves and other debris. Bark needs topping up at least annually, and both gravel and bark often find their way onto lawns, giving you a raking job before you mow. However, they are still relatively easy surfaces to maintain. (For more on hard surfaces, *see* pages 25–7 and 54–5.)

Gravel and raised decking provide interest in this small space and are good easy-care choices for the area around the house; the distant lawn receives less 'traffic'.

Don't forget

Gravel and bark are more environmentally friendly than paving or concrete. Water drains through them easily, while it runs off solid surfaces, sometimes causing flooding.

The vertical surfaces

Fences, walls, pergolas and arches all come under the heading of vertical surfaces, and from year to year most need hardly any maintenance at all. Of course, there is wear and tear and eventually most walls need painting or repointing and fences, pergolas and arches will require replacing or fixing. However, aside from an annual cleaning session for painted surfaces if you feel so inclined, most of these will easily go between five and ten years without needing any attention at all.

The big attention-seeker among vertical surfaces is the hedge, particularly a formal one. Most formal hedges need at least one trim a year, many should really have two and, in between times, they often begin to look rather untidy after a couple of months in the summer. On the plus side, hedges are very important for wildlife, and some can be allowed to become a little more informal, particularly the flowering kind. It all depends on whether you are keener on having less work or a really neat garden. (For more on vertical surfaces, *see* pages 28–9.)

Water

All gardens benefit from having a water feature or pond, and once set up most don't need a great deal of looking after. If you're considering introducing water to the garden and don't want to spend much time on maintenance, think big. A large, healthy, informal pond is more or less self-sustaining and therefore very undemanding; at the other end of the scale, a small water feature in a pot will need cleaning out almost

A pergola is an attractive addition to any garden, providing a strong focal point and plenty of vertical interest, as well as a sturdy, low-maintenance support for plants.

every week, especially in summer. This is because small bodies of water are considerably more susceptible to temperature changes, and warm water encourages algal growth.

A pond also has other benefits, because it encourages a variety of wildlife into your garden and these frogs, newts, toads, hedgehogs and birds will help you to keep your nuisance slug, snail and insect populations at bay. However, don't despair if you can't fit an Olympic-size pool in your garden: wildlife is really not too particular and will be attracted to any area of water, no matter how small.

Select your pond plants with care. As is the case elsewhere in the garden, the types of plants suitable for ponds can be high or low maintenance. Reeds can be invasive and tend to be very vigorous; they require an annual chop back, while most water lilies are much slower to spread and need dividing only every third year or so. (For more on water, *see* pages 30–1 and 56–7.)

Assessing your needs

To create a garden that meets your needs, think very carefully about how you like to spend time at weekends. Try to be really honest with yourself and be realistic about how much time you're prepared to commit to working in the garden. Use this information to come up with a sensible plan of action.

Now and in the future

There are two main reasons why most of us want to have a garden that can be kept under control in a few hours at the weekend: either we have too much to do elsewhere, or we have physical restrictions that prevent us from doing too much gardening. Either way, the aim is the same, but there may be long-term differences. For example, if you have a young family and a full-time job, your immediate needs are for an easy-care garden, but there is every chance you might like to have the option of expanding its potential in the future. On the other hand, if you're more mature and are finding gardening an increasing chore, but still want an outdoor space you can enjoy, you'll need more permanent simplicity. These considerations are important, since they can affect how much you want to spend on your plans and how far you're prepared to go in remodelling your garden.

Do you enjoy gardening?

It may seem an odd question, but it does have a bearing on the sort of garden you ought to end up with. Someone who isn't really interested in tending plants yet wants to have an attractive outdoor space will need to devote a larger area to hard landscaping than to flower beds, while still allowing for some plants that will more or less take care of themselves (see pages 64–91). At the other end of the spectrum, if you enjoy tending plants you'll still have to consider hard surfaces but you can keep these to a minimum and be a little more adventurous with your plant choices.

What do you use your garden for?

Finally, ask yourself what you want to do in your garden. A space for children will be different from one wholly for adults; if you like a place to sit quietly and contemplate, it will be quite different from an outdoor 'room' for entertaining. The checklist opposite will help you to clarify what you want to get out of your garden. Spend some time thinking carefully about it, and you're more likely to be delighted with the results.

Don't forget

If your garden is too big for you, consider contacting Landshare (www.landshare.com). This is an organization that puts those who have land to share in contact with those who need it, primarily for growing food.

This garden has been designed for meditation and contemplation. Water, gravel, stone, wood and lush foliage plants blend to create a peaceful scene.

Questionnaire

The questions below will prompt you to consider how to make your garden easy to care for, taking into account your circumstances, budget and timescale. It should help you to focus on the elements that make up a low-maintenance garden and will lead you to the pages in this book where you can find the relevant information.

Are you designing a low-maintenance garden from scratch?

Think about what style of garden would suit you and discover how to plan a new garden that will need minimal maintenance, leaving you free to relax and enjoy it at weekends.

See:

• What's your style? pages 14–17
• Designing an easy-care garden, pages 18–19

Are you prepared to make some basic structural improvements that will make your garden easier to look after in the longer term?

There are several simple (not necessarily expensive) improvements that you can make now that will save you a great deal of time and/or labour in the future. If you don't want to spend your weekends doing DIY, it's well worth hiring a professional to do the work for you, particularly if you're planning to stay put for years to come.

See:

• Patios, paths and steps, pages 25–7
• Fences, walls, hedges and structures, pages 28–9
• Water, pages 30–1 and 56–7 (Project: Wildlife pond)
• Raised beds, pages 34 and 52–3 (Project: Raised vegetable bed)
• Project: Wildflower mini-meadow, pages 48–9
• Project: Gravel bed, pages 50–1
• Project: Paved herb garden, pages 54–5

Do you want to grow a selection of beautiful plants that require very little maintenance and can more or less look after themselves?

There are plenty of ways you can make your garden easier to care for, simply by selecting some low-maintenance plants, putting them in the right place and adopting certain gardening techniques to ensure they remain healthy and trouble-free.

See:

• Recommended easy-care plants, pages 64–91
• Beds and borders, pages 32–3
• Containers, pages 35–6
• The lawn, pages 22–4
• Plant care and maintenance, pages 37–45
• Challenging sites, pages 58–63

What's your style?

When designing any garden, it helps to plan it with a finished 'look' in mind, since so many of the key features, such as the hard landscaping and the plants, will be influenced by your preferences. It can be tricky to choose a style – particularly if you're new to gardening – but some of the most popular ones are described here, which may help you decide.

Bear in mind you'll be happiest with a garden that reflects something of your personality and taste – you may prefer symmetry and order or feel more comfortable with a relaxed, informal 'muddle'. Also, think about the style of building that you live in and its setting – is it traditional or modern, urban or rural? The various maintenance requirements of the garden styles are outlined here too, so consider how much time you're prepared to spend on gardening before making any decisions.

Woodland

A woodland garden consists of trees, perhaps with an understorey of shrubs and some smaller plants. If it's properly planted, and with a sensible layout that includes plenty of room to mow grass or for wide bark paths, this is one of the easiest of all garden styles to look after and is a very good way of filling ground that is at some distance from the house.

Well-spaced (and initially well-staked) trees need very little in the way of maintenance, and the shade they cast tends to suppress much in the way of growth underneath, so doing away with the need for endless weeding. Bulbs and other spring flowers grow well beneath trees. They're very easy to look after and naturalize happily in grass, which can be kept in check with a weekly mow. In a large area, you could use a ride-on mower. Hard surfaces can be limited to areas near the house.

Even if you have quite a small garden, you can suggest woodland in one corner with just one or two trees and some well-placed shrubs.

Urban jungle

An exotic jungle made up of large plants with big leaves and lush growth is the urban answer to a woodland garden. Although many true jungle plants cannot survive winter outside, there are plenty of hardy alternatives that look the part. The dense leaf canopy suppresses weeds underneath, and covering the ground around taller plants with bark chippings or gravel used as a mulch will reduce maintenance work. Gravel can also be used for paths in an urban jungle garden, or you may consider decking.

Don't forget

It is perfectly possible to combine different styles within one garden provided you plan it carefully. For instance, you could divide your garden into a series of distinct spaces, or 'rooms', with a formal terrace located near the house and a wildlife haven in a quiet corner.

In this imaginative woodland planting, the white flowers of the viburnum are set off perfectly by the white bark of the birch trees.

In this jungle-themed garden, a secluded patio is surrounded by hardy yuccas and phormiums, with flowers provided by tender cannas.

Hardy, jungle-like plants include various bamboos, *Fatsia japonica*, *Griselinia littoralis* and ferns. A word of caution about bamboos: choose clump-forming varieties and, if you plant them in the ground, keep an eye out for 'canes' that are growing horizontally. These are the rhizomes by which most bamboos spread and they can go a long way; remove them if they're going in the wrong direction or too far. Bamboos benefit from a good annual tidy-up.

Cottage gardens

True cottage gardens are not low maintenance. The relaxed, casual, colour-filled look actually takes a good deal of work: there are annual flowers and vegetables to grow from seed, plant, dead-head, remove and replace. However, it is possible to borrow many of the stylistic ideas found in a traditional cottage garden, such as brick paths, wooden fences and rustic pergolas, and create something that looks fairly authentic.

You will still need lots of colour, and the best way to get this is to fill the plot with a selection of cottage-garden-type plants that are easy to look after. There are many, including informal flowering shrubs such as hydrangeas, viburnums and potentillas, and you can replace the annuals with perennials, such as hellebores, phlox and geraniums. If you want roses, pick modern, disease-resistant varieties (*see* pages 77–8).

Seaside setting

If you don't want lots of plants and like the idea of setting a scene, a seaside garden might be the answer. Rope, railway sleepers, a raised deck built near the house and contoured landscaping covered with gravel and pebbles or sand will go a long way towards creating the right sort of ambience. You could even add a shed painted in beach-hut colours.

No one expects to see numerous lush plants at the seaside: a selection of grasses, salt-tolerant and wind-resistant shrubs, and a few tough flowering perennials or annuals will help to complete the look. Even in the middle of a town, a seaside garden can be very effective and, once in place, not very much work to maintain.

Railway sleepers, driftwood, pebbles and low-growing grasses and succulents suggest a seaside setting.

Wildlife haven

Woody, leafy plants with plenty of upper and undergrowth are very popular with many animals and insects, so variations of a woodland garden, preferably with the addition of some flowering shrubs and other flowering plants, will attract wildlife. You can ensure success by building a wildlife pond (*see* pages 56–7), which will provide birds, frogs, toads, dragonflies and so on with water and a source of food. Such a garden also offers the excuse not to be too up to scratch with your maintenance, since insects like nesting in old pieces of wood and feeding on weed flowers, while birds are happy to polish off those that become pests, such as aphids and caterpillars. The whole idea of a wildlife garden is that it is relaxed and natural, and left to its own devices as much as possible.

Traditional formal

This type of garden is typified by the parterre, with its geometric and symmetrical pattern of paths and low, clipped hedges that create compartments for displaying groups of the same sorts of plants. There's no need to stick to traditional box hedging or topiary centrepieces, as long as the planting overall has a formal feel.

A whole garden, even a small one, given up to this style is hard work, because its success relies on the neatness of the hedges and the uniformity of the plants within them. However, if you like the idea of symmetry and tidiness, you'll enjoy the process of producing it and will be happy to devote at least part of your weekend to it.

If you want a traditional formal garden but don't have a lot of time for maintaining it, one approach is to have a small formal area that can be kept under control with ease and then to have a more relaxed style for the rest of the garden.

Alternatively, you can add some structural formality to a wholly informal garden, say in a cottage-garden style, by introducing just a few formal plants. Topiary is a popular way of doing this; cones or balls are good. 'Globe' bay or olive trees are readily available, and there are a number of evergreen shrubs, including pittosporum, that can be clipped into tall cone shapes. All these will need only a light trim now and then to maintain their shape.

Modern

The essence of a contemporary garden is well-ordered hard landscaping into which a range of carefully chosen plants has been placed; it is light and clutter-free.

'Modern' plants are usually architectural, with a distinctive, strong shape. They have a long season of interest, and are generally well behaved. Grasses are much used, their soft forms contrasting with big, spiky plants. Slim, elegant trees are also a feature of modern gardens, particularly white-stemmed birches (*Betula utilis* var. *jacquemontii*), which look good in winter. Colour schemes are cool, perhaps green, white and silver, or black-purple contrasting with lime green.

Colour can also be provided by rendered and painted walls and

This informal garden is designed to attract wildlife, with dense planting and plenty of nectar-rich flowers.

Restrained use of colour and an emphasis on clean horizontal and vertical lines are among the key elements of many modern-style gardens.

ceramic, fibreglass, concrete or metal containers. A modern garden may well have a tidy water feature, perhaps with a waterfall, and often some discreetly installed lighting. Furniture will be nothing if not contemporary in design.

A well-designed modern garden should be fairly easy to care for, so long as easy-care plants have been selected. However, to maintain that essential crisp look, you do need to keep the plants in good condition with regular watering, feeding and dead-heading.

Family gardens

Most garden styles are suitable for children, although formal gardens are less likely to appeal to them and will have fewer places for typical outdoor games. If you have room, create a specific space for your children to play in, as well as somewhere they can grow plants. With a little thought, such spaces can be adapted as the children grow, eventually being merged into the adult garden.

Minimalist

A minimalist garden is a modern-style garden that has been pared to the bone, with the emphasis very much on sleek landscaping materials rather than plants.

The minimalist style is often used to good effect in small, awkward spaces, for instance in a basement courtyard or a gap between high walls. There may be just one or two cleverly placed plants to provide something living to look at while the rest of the area is occupied with sharply defined shapes made from wood, concrete or stone. A larger space may include a formal pool or very neatly trimmed area of grass.

A minimalist garden requires firm commitment to the belief that less is more, and it is not for the gardener addicted to plants.

Prairie

Suitable for large, open spaces, and particularly for exposed situations, this contemporary, low-maintenance style of planting includes tall grasses and wind- and drought-tolerant perennial plants such as penstemons, echinaceas, heleniums and *Sedum spectabile*, planted *en masse* in large swathes and drifts.

Prairie gardens look their best in late summer, when most of these plants are performing, and when frost-rimed in winter. Drifts of plants chosen for their flowers can be a bit dull when these go over – but then prairie planting is really more about light, movement and texture than colour. Densely planted, these gardens need little weeding, and if drought-tolerant plants are chosen, no watering once established.

Designing an easy-care garden

Whatever sort of garden you want, you need to think of it as a whole to start with, even if you plan to create it over several years. Planning it all at once allows you to decide where the major elements, such as paths, patios and flower beds, will go and how they will relate to each other. And this is the best way to ensure that you have the most straightforward and easy-to-look-after garden, not just for now but also in the future.

Making a plan

If you've read this far you'll know the elements in a garden that take the most looking after, and you should be more aware of the workload your chosen style might create. Now you need to put the two together and come up with a garden that you will enjoy spending time in but that

Take your time when doing any sort of garden design. Look in books for ideas and do sketches to see whether they might work in your space.

won't make you feel harassed if you can't get into it for a couple of weekends. It's a good idea to make a detailed plan of your proposed garden to help you visualize the proportion of open space to planting and so you can see exactly what goes where.

First, measure the perimeter of your garden accurately using a long tape measure, then transfer the measurements onto a scale diagram. Use graph paper and choose a simple scale, such as 1cm = 1 metre or 50cm (that

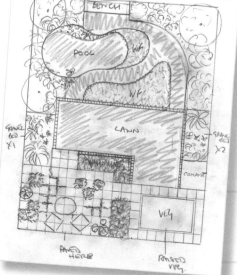

A scale drawing is an excellent way to check that you can include everything you want, that it all fits together well and looks good, too.

is, 1cm on the plan = 1m or 50cm on the ground). Next, measure and mark any existing features that will remain in the garden, such as paths, sheds, manhole covers and trees or shrubs you're going to keep. Again, transfer these to the scale drawing.

Once you have your scale drawing, make photocopies of the plan. You

Don't forget

If you find it difficult to work on paper, you could use one of the computer-aided design programmes available. Alternatively, go out into the garden with a length of hosepipe or pegs and string and play with shapes for the lawn, patio, path and so on.

can then sketch in your ideas for how you'd like the garden to look in the future. Keep making adjustments until you're happy with the design.

The key garden elements

The hard landscaping will form the skeleton of the garden and is a good starting point for your design, as it will determine the positions of other features. Design it carefully, so it will be easy to look after and a pleasure to use. Think about its style in relation to your house style, as well as the style of the garden you want to create. Take care with size and scale. Make paths a sensible width for wheelbarrows and pedestrians, and ensure your patio will take a table and chairs with ease (*see* chart, right). It's always better to have too much space than too little.

The shape of the lawn depends to a certain extent on the hard landscaping and the flower beds, since they're all interconnected. However, don't allow the lawn to become a squiggly green space squeezed in between everything else. Keep the shape simple, for mowing, and make sure it's large enough to mow with ease.

Think about the size of beds and borders, too. Make sure they're a sensible size: too small and the plants will need constant cutting back (also, you won't be able to include as many plants of different heights for interest). Raised beds are often easier to maintain than ground-level beds, as you can sit on their edges and weed with ease. Also, the soil is looser and drains more freely. (For more on raised beds, *see* pages 34 and 52–3.)

If you're going to have a pond or water feature of any size, factor it in very early on. Make sure you'll be able to fill it easily and top it up as necessary. If you want a fountain, you'll need to allow for electricity and the skills of an electrician, too. Informal ponds are usually less labour-intensive and more self-sustaining than formal ones. Make sure your pond can be walked right around, to make maintenance easier.

The utilities

While you're thinking about the hard landscaping, keep in mind the utilitarian parts of the garden, such as a shed, washing line and so on. You might even want to allow for a greenhouse, depending on where your gardening interests lie. Think about how you're going to get to each place – you'll need a good path – and how you are going to use it. For example, if you want to store your mower in the shed, make sure there's plenty of room to manoeuvre it in and out. Struggling with tools is a very annoying waste of time when you have only half an hour to spare.

An outdoor tap is always going to come in handy and, even in a small garden, will save a lot of work running in and out of the house to fill watering cans. Look for places to install water butts. If you can have several discreetly placed around the garden it reduces walking distance in the summer. Having several watering cans, at least one for each water source, is also a good idea.

Getting the dimensions right

It's crucial to get the dimensions of the key elements right in a garden, particularly if it's to be as labour-saving as possible. If a lawn is tiny, it will be difficult to manoeuvre the mower; if borders are too narrow, you'll need to cut back plants regularly; and if raised beds are too wide you'll have difficulty stretching across to maintain them. Below are some measurements to consider at the planning stage.

GARDEN FEATURE	RECOMMENDED MEASUREMENTS
Borders and beds	**Minimum width:** 1.2–1.5m (4–5ft)
	Maximum width: the wider the better, but you may need stepping stones to allow access for maintenance
Raised bed	**Maximum width:** bed you can access from one side only 75cm (2½ft); bed you can access from both sides 1.5m (5ft)
	Minimum height: 45cm (18in); ideally 60–90cm (2–3ft)
Lawn	**Minimum size:** 3 x 3m (10 x 10ft)
Patio/dining area	**For two people sitting at a table (and chairs):** paved area minimum 2.5 x 1.5m (8 x 5ft)
	For six people (round table and chairs): paved area minimum 3.5 x 3.5m (12 x 12ft)
	For eight people (rectangular table and chairs): paved area minimum 4.5 x 3.5m (15 x 12ft)
Paths	**For one person walking:** 60cm (2ft)
	For two people walking: 1.2m (4ft)
	For a wheelchair: 1.2m (4ft) to allow for easy turnaround
	For a wheelbarrow: minimum width 60cm (2ft)

Making a labour-saving garden

One of the basic principles of an easy-care garden is if you put in a little time and effort at key times you'll make life a lot easier for yourself in the long run. As this section shows, making a few small improvements or adopting gardening techniques that reduce or eliminate labour-intensive jobs, such as digging and weeding, really can make a difference. The chapter ends with five simple projects that if implemented now will considerably reduce your workload in the future. For a good selection of plants that require very little input, *see* the Recommended easy-care plants directory (pages 64–91).

Minimizing maintenance

Whatever style of garden you're hoping to create, aim to include a combination of soft and hard surfaces as well as a mixture of flat and vertical ones. In order to keep your workload to a minimum, balance high-maintenance decorative features, such as flower borders, with simpler, lower-maintenance areas, for instance a paved patio or a lawn. If you get the balance right, you'll have an inviting, usable and easy-care outdoor living space.

Selecting materials

Once you've decided on the various improvements or alterations, always buy the best materials that you can afford. This is particularly important when you can't always be out in the garden mending and tending. Go for high-quality materials that will look good and last a long time.

If you want to lay a new patio or put up a pergola, choose a design that you really like, and if you can't be sure you can do a good job of installing it, or if you don't enjoy DIY, get a professional in. There is little point in wasting days trying to erect a pergola or lay paving if the results are shoddy or you need to redo the work later.

Use the best tools

All garden work is considerably more enjoyable when you use good-quality tools that suit your height, strength and so on. Blunt secateurs or a heavy, uncomfortable border fork will not encourage you to get out into the garden. The same goes for mechanical equipment. If the mower doesn't always start first time, don't spend all of Saturday afternoon in the shed with your hands covered in oil – get it properly serviced or consider replacing it.

When well fed, clematis are great performers. This one is teamed with tall purple *Verbena bonariensis*, which rarely needs staking, and bright pink *Lychnis coronaria* – easy in a dry spot.

Organizing your time

Even if you have only a couple of hours to spare at the weekend, you can still get plenty done and keep your garden looking good. A word of advice for those who have limited time: each weekend try to do at least one job that really *needs* doing and one that you positively *like* doing. Following this advice should mean that as well as feeling you've achieved something, you get to enjoy your precious time out in the garden. Be realistic about what you can and cannot do, and never try to do too much – gardening should be a pleasure, not a chore.

Don't forget

The key to a successful, easy-care weekend garden is to plan ahead and make changes to reduce the number of tasks you'll need to carry out in the future. It is not about cutting down on time spent on the essential jobs, such as mowing or weeding.

The lawn

Most people couldn't imagine a garden without a lawn – a lush green expanse that is not only pleasing to the eye but also provides a wonderfully soft surface to sit, lie, play and walk on. Yet for the harried weekend gardener who wants a neat, tidy plot, the lawn can become symbolic of a neglected garden, seemingly full of unfinished tasks. However, there are ways to have a beautiful lawn without the hassle, if you're prepared to put up with a few imperfections.

Good-quality turf provides an almost instant lawn, although you still have to prepare the ground thoroughly.

Creating a new lawn

To make your lawn easy to look after, opt for a simple, geometrical shape or, for something less formal, soft, long curves. Avoid having any oddly shaped corners that are hard to negotiate or grass paths that are narrower than the mower. Gently flowing curves are more forgiving than a circle or rectangle, as any imperfections are not so visible; they also enable flexibility with the routes of nearby paths and the shapes of adjacent flower beds.

Preparing the ground

When creating a new lawn, it's vital that you prepare the ground thoroughly – work put in now will be more than repaid later. A flat bed of fertile soil will provide your new grass with an excellent start, unless

Seed or turf?

For the weekend gardener, turf is usually the better option. It can be laid almost all year round, covers the ground completely (so reducing weed growth) and can be walked on within three weeks or so. However, you have more choice if you buy seed, since you can select a mix for a particular use, such as play areas or shady sites. There are also mixes that contain microclover, which has tiny leaves that stay green even in drought conditions and requires less feeding. Both turf and seed need regular watering until they are well established.

you decide to have a wildflower meadow, which does not require fertile soil (*see* pages 48–9).

Clear the area and dig the soil to a spade's depth. Rake the surface and remove any large stones or other debris. Trample and rake several times to get the soil surface as fine and level as possible. Check for hollows and high ground, and transfer soil between the two if necessary. Scatter grass fertilizer over the area to help your new lawn to

A small lawn can be the centrepiece of a garden. This one has mowing edges, which will make mowing it much easier.

establish. Finally, tread over every inch of the soil to ensure it settles evenly and rake gently one last time. You are now ready to lay turf or sow grass seed.

Mowing

Mowing is unavoidable, and as a general rule needs carrying out weekly between mid-spring and mid-autumn, although in a damp summer it may need a midweek cut too. Not only does regular mowing keep the lawn looking neat, it also prevents weeds from spreading.

Try to keep the height of the grass the same throughout the growing season, and don't make the mistake of trying to save time by cutting the grass very short in order to mow less frequently, as this will only ruin the

Don't forget

Even if you prepare properly, there is always going to be some maintenance involved in a lawn; if you can't afford the time involved in mowing and feeding, consider replacing it with a hard surface such as paving or gravel (see pages 25–7, 50–1 and 54–5) or artificial grass.

lawn. The cutting height should be about 2.5cm (1in), except for the first cut in spring, which should be slightly higher. (*See also* box, below.)

Neat edges

One of the most labour-intensive lawn tasks is maintaining the edges. These crumble and the grass grows out into borders. It is impossible to mow unprotected edges, so they need to be regularly trimmed with a strimmer (which is messy and noisy) or by hand (which is back-breaking and slow). Also, every year the edges need to be cut back into shape. It is all so much easier if you have a permanent edge around the lawn.

The best sort of mowing edge is one that is wide enough to take the wheels of a lawn mower and is flush with the level of the lawn. You can buy specially designed edges of concrete or plastic, but bricks or concrete setts are equally suitable. Upright metal strips or wooden edges provide definition but do not reduce trimming work.

Feeding

Grass that is frequently cut expends a lot of energy in regrowth, so it needs lots of food. For the weekend gardener, it makes sense to use a long-lasting fertilizer formulated for your soil type; some last for up to six months. They may cost more, but they save time and ensure a good-looking lawn all year round.

The quickest way to feed a lawn is to use granules. You can use a special distributor that spreads these evenly over the lawn, but for most family lawns scattering is fine. Choose a day when rain is forecast, or you'll have to water them in.

To water or not to water ...

A new lawn will need regular watering (ideally in the evening), but avoid watering an established lawn. In very dry weather, mow less frequently (longer grass will shade its own roots) and use a higher cut to reduce stress on the grass. Also, leave the clippings on the lawn as a mulch to retain moisture (do this for a few weeks only). Regular feeding and weeding will help the grass to grow vigorously and reduce competition for the available water.

HOW TO lay a mowing edge

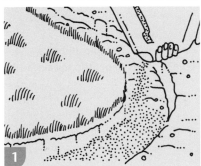

1

Dig a shallow trench around the lawn's perimeter. Make it deep enough for the edging stones plus a foundation layer of sharp sand about 2.5cm (1in) deep. Put the sand into the trench and tamp it level.

2

Start laying the edging stones about 6mm (¼in) apart. Check that each is flush with the one beside it and that they are at the same height as the lawn. Use a spirit level to check that they are all level.

3

Brush a slightly damp grouting mix between the gaps, then finish the joints with a pointing tool (*see* step 4, page 55). Once the mix has set, fill gaps between your new edge and the lawn with soil.

Lawn makeover

If you have an established lawn that looks as if it could do with some help, you could consider a revamp. Unless your lawn is huge, a revamp is easily undertaken over a weekend and it will reduce maintenance in the long term. Revamps are best done in autumn, but in spring a dose of fertilizer will do wonders. Once your lawn is in good health, keep it that way by regular mowing and feeding.

Three steps for healthy grass

The first thing to consider is the health of the grass. Devote a few hours to removing any moss and dead grass (called thatch) using a spring-tine rake (*see* 1). Known as scarifying, this involves deep raking and is hard work, but you can hire a powered lawn rake.

Next, aerate the lawn by driving a garden fork about 7–15cm (3–6in) into the soil at 15–20cm (6–8in) intervals (*see* 2). You could either do the whole lawn or, if you're short of time, focus on those areas that are particularly compacted, perhaps where you walk a lot or where the children play. Aerating will allow air into the grass roots so the lawn can grow again.

If you have the time, it's well worth following aerating and scarifying with top-dressing, which acts as a general tonic as well as helping to improve drainage on heavy soils. The top-dressing is a mix of good-quality topsoil, sand and humus-rich material that you spread thinly over the surface of the lawn – you should still be able to see the grass blades. Use the rake to spread it, easing it into holes made during aeration (*see* 3).

Making the lawn level

Top-dressing should help to get rid of any small hollows, but deal with obvious lumps and larger hollows in your lawn by peeling back the turf in the affected area. Fill hollows with a soil-and-compost mix, treading it down to ensure it doesn't settle below the lawn level. Remove whatever is causing the lump and loosen the soil around it. Replace the turf and water well until the grass has re-established.

Filling bare patches

You may find that you have bare patches in the lawn. If so, it's quick and easy to reseed. Prick the area with a garden fork, rake the surface and then sow seed thinly and water. Keep off the lawn until the seed has germinated and is growing strongly.

To returf, remove the dead patch, leaving a square or rectangular shape. Dig lightly over the exposed surface and water well. Lay the new turves over the area, cutting them to fit as closely as possible. Firm them down and fill any gaps with fine sand. Water them in.

Don't forget

A well-tended lawn will enhance the whole garden, while a neglected one will detract from even the most beautiful garden. Spending just a few hours a year on lawn care can make all the difference and will give you a lawn you can be proud of.

Follow these steps for a healthier, more attractive lawn.

① Use a spring-tine rake to scratch up moss and dead grass.

② Aerate the soil by making holes with a fork.

③ Rake top-dressing over the grass to condition the soil beneath.

Patios, paths and steps

Once they're installed, hard surfaces, such as patios, paths and steps, require very little in the way of maintenance; it's therefore a good idea to include at least one or two areas of hard landscaping in your weekend garden. As well as making a valuable contribution to a garden's appearance and the ways it can be used, the other major attraction of surfaced areas is that they provide places to sit and enjoy the garden.

Gravel

Gravel is a very versatile material that is easy to lay and is suitable for using in a great number of situations, from tiny spaces to large expanses. It is ideal for paths and driveways and can also be used for seating areas, although paving and decking are better for permanent dining areas, providing a more stable base. Gravel has a uniform colour and appearance that automatically makes a space look neater.

Gravel can also be used as an attractive background for planting (*see* pages 50–1). With a little imagination, you can use it to create a variety of effects in the garden, including a dried-out stream bed, a shingle river bank, a rough mountain scree or a pebbly beach.

A combination of gravel and paving slabs creates a practical, informal path that is also an attractive feature in its own right.

There are many types of stone chippings available, including flint, granite, limestone and slate, and they come in a variety of sizes and colours, from purple-blue and golden yellow to nearly white. If gravel is laid over a weedproof membrane or applied as a deep layer, it will help to suppress weeds and, unlike paving or decking, gravel does not become

Blue slate chippings and black-painted raised beds emphasize the Japanese style of this little corner.

Don't forget

Gravel has a tendency to spread into other parts of the garden, so you may need to confine it with edging, especially near grass, since gravel and lawn mowers do not mix.

slippery in shady areas. An annual raking to remove debris and discourage weeds should ensure it remains looking smart; it might also need topping up every few years. Gravel is a good environmentally friendly choice (*see* page 10).

Decking

Decking is a very attractive and practical surface that can be used to create patios, terraces and paths. It has the great advantage over paving in that it can be put directly over uneven or sloping ground, or over

Don't forget

If you're buying decking, make sure the timber comes from a properly managed source – such woods are usually clearly marked.

an existing hard surface, avoiding the need for any major earthworks. Decking is easy to cut to fit almost any space and can be finished with a straight edge or a curve. You can buy it as a pre-designed flatpack, with everything you need including balustrades and steps, or customize it for your own particular needs.

Decking is not as long-lasting as paving, and requires quite a bit more maintenance, but it is much quicker to install. For example, you could easily build a large deck over a weekend. Once in place, it will require an annual scrub or pressure-wash and should also be restained in order to keep the wood in the best condition possible, even if it has been treated prior to purchase. Like

paving, it can become slippery in shaded situations, but you could combat this by using special finishes or even by stapling fine chicken-wire mesh over the affected area.

Pavers, bricks and setts

For most patios, paths and other hard surfaces, there is little to beat paving stones. They come in such a wide range of shapes, sizes and colours you're bound to find one to fit in with your house style and the character of your garden.

Well-laid paved areas are almost maintenance-free, apart from the odd sweep clean; design them without awkward corners where the broom won't reach. It's best to use paving in moderation: large, flat areas of concrete or brick can be very stark and uninviting. If you don't want a solid paved area, you can leave out some pavers and use the space as growing pockets (*see* pages 54–5). Alternatively, pavers can be combined with bricks, setts or even gravel. Setts are used in a similar way to bricks, but their curved edges mean they usually produce a slightly uneven surface and therefore an olde-worlde feel. They are particularly effective if you want to create curved patterns and shapes in your paved area.

A small inset of bricks creates additional interest in a large expanse of paving, which is also softened by the overhanging shrubs.

Shady areas

Shaded patios or paths may become slippery with algae and moss and will need pressure-washing or scrubbing about once a year to ensure they don't become dangerous. You can reduce this problem by combining paved surfaces with gravel, so you can walk on the gravel when the paving is wet, or by using gravel on its own in shady spots.

Brick and paving patterns

Depending on how you lay your bricks or slabs, you can create a variety of effects. Pick your pattern to make the most of your space. Looking across a herringbone layout in the direction of the zigzag shortens and widens the area; looking along the zigzag lengthens and narrows it. A path of bricks laid lengthways looks longer than if laid crossways.

Paving can be laid with the joints (courses) matching or staggered. Matching courses make a bold pattern, suitable for a modern or formal garden. Staggered joints are softer on the eye and foreshorten the distance across them. Laying paving crossways, so it becomes diamonds with triangular inserts, increases the feeling of space.

Natural stone flags (and their imitations) come in a variety of different-sized rectangles and squares, and are usually laid in a seemingly irregular way, called a 'random' pattern. The subtle effect is most suitable for informal styles of garden.

Choose a style that will suit your particular space.

① Herringbone makes a classic, formal pattern.

② Parquet is ideal for small areas.

③ Latticework makes use of half-bricks as well as whole ones.

④ Natural stone paving slabs are usually laid in 'random' patterns.

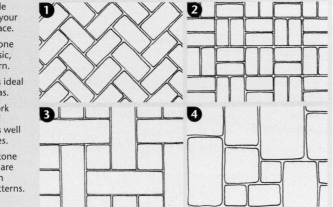

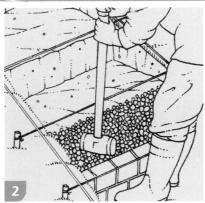

Steps

Steps are often a necessity, but they can also be used as a design feature. Even if you have a flat garden, it's worth adding a step or two, as you'll automatically make the space look a lot more interesting, particularly if you combine them with a raised bed. Even a flight of steps that leads nowhere but the shed offers you the chance to drape a plant over them or add an ornamental handrail. They are often made from bricks and paving slabs, but railway sleepers or half-logs are also an option. They need little aftercare, but contribute a lot to the ambience of the garden.

Ideally, risers for outdoor steps should be not more than 10–15cm (4–6in) high, and treads should be not less than 30cm (12in) from front to back. There should be a very slight fall (1cm/½in) to the nosing to ensure rapid water runoff.

HOW TO make steps

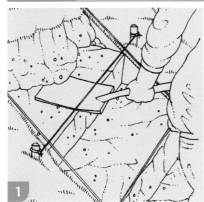

1 Mark out the sides of the steps and the front of each tread using string and some wooden pegs. Ideally, the treads should be a minimum of 30cm (12in) from front to back, but this depends on your materials and the steepness of the slope. Using a spade, dig out the shapes of the steps and then compact the soil.

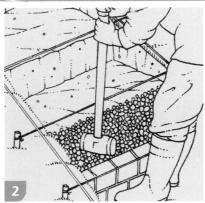

2 Build the steps from the bottom up. Start by creating a footing, which is a layer of hardcore topped with a layer of concrete, to support the first riser. Allow this to set before building the first riser. Check its alignment with a spirit level. Once the riser has set, fill the area behind it with hardcore. Compact and level this.

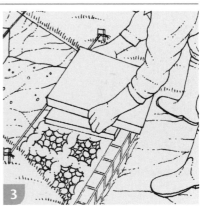

3 Place mortar on the riser and hardcore and position the tread. Again, allow the mortar to set, then build the next riser on the back of the tread. Continue until you reach the top, then brush grouting mix (see step 4, page 55) between the treads to finish. Refill gaps around the edges of the steps with soil (you can turf or plant them later).

Fences, walls, hedges and structures

There are many vertical elements in a garden – fences, walls and hedges, for instance, or decorative structures, such as pergolas and arches. All these add height and visual interest as well as providing privacy and altering the feeling of space and enclosure. It's easy to choose boundaries and decorative structures that require little in the way of maintenance.

Fences

Fences are cheap and quick to install, and you can easily do it yourself over a weekend. (Erect fence posts in the same way as the posts for raised beds, *see* pages 52–3.) You can embellish them with a panel of trellis along the top and can paint them if you wish. However, remember that paint must be renewed every two or three years or so, and looks terrible when it starts to chip off, whereas good-quality, pressure-treated wood ages to a lovely silver-grey and needs virtually no maintenance. It is easy to fix frames for climbing plants to fences and then the plants provide all the decoration you need.

Walls

Walls form the most permanent boundary and are very attractive as well as secure and low maintenance. If you're lucky enough to have walled boundaries, make the most of them by giving them a facelift (if they need it) and then using them as part of the framework of the garden. Walls can be hung with trellis or other plant-climbing frames, but they also make a suitable surface for displaying garden ornaments, such as intricate metalwork or pottery.

If you're planning to live in the same place for a reasonable time and can afford the expense, it is well worth considering building a walled boundary. Walls can be made from blocks, which are usually rendered, or bricks. It is vital that they're properly built, especially if you want something of a reasonable height, so you might want to get a professional to do the work for you. Always finish walls with a layer of coping, because this helps to keep out water, which can cause cracking and splitting.

Hedges

Hedges make a beautiful living boundary and provide a wonderful habitat for wildlife; they also make a good barrier against noise, wind and dust. Their main drawbacks are that they take up more space than walls and fences and some require a lot of clipping, especially formal hedges. However, there are many hedging plants that don't require much work and would be perfectly suitable for the time-pressed weekend gardener.

If planting a hedge, reduce the future workload by choosing either slow-growing or informal flowering plants. Slow-growing hedges need

Don't forget

Pressure-treated cedar and oak are among the most hardwearing of timbers and are ideal for the low-maintenance garden.

Brick walls make lovely features and are low maintenance. Here, decorative fence panels have ensured additional privacy.

This informal hedge is made from *Rosa rugosa* varieties. Fragrant and long-flowering, they can be severely pruned when necessary.

trimming only once a year, and informal flowering hedges don't need any regular clipping or trimming at all; just prune back overlong or untidy shoots if necessary. You could have a hedge of mixed shrubs, including plants that have different flowering times or produce colourful foliage as well as flowers and fruit, to provide year-round interest.

It's best to avoid formal hedges that need clipping several times a year, for example box (*Buxus*), yew (*Taxus*), privet (*Ligustrum*) and fast-growing conifers including *Cuprocyparis leylandii*. If you do have a formal hedge and don't want to replace it, make sure you don't let it grow taller than 1.8m (6ft), as clipping will be a lot more difficult if some of the hedge is out of reach.

Don't forget

The best informal hedges need space to expand widthways. Allow at least 2m (6ft) or more if you have the room and ideally leave 30–60cm (12–24in) between plants.

Easy-care hedging plants

Berberis (most)
Corylus avellana
Crataegus
Elaeagnus pungens 'Maculata'
Escallonia
Griselinia littoralis
Pyracantha
Rosa rugosa
Viburnum opulus

Garden structures

Vertical structures, such as pergolas, arches, arbours, obelisks, wigwams, rustic tripods and pillars, provide plenty of visual interest in the garden without many maintenance concerns. As well as being very attractive and making striking focal points, they are also extremely useful, because they provide a support for climbing plants, often create places for sitting, and can be used to increase your privacy and sense of enclosure.

For a weekend gardener, their other selling point is that they occupy space that might otherwise require maintenance. For example,

imagine a pergola positioned over an informal gravelled area and with a vigorous clematis or vine trained over the top. The space taken up by this arrangement is the equivalent of quite a large flower bed, but there is only one plant to look after and the gravel suppresses all weeds. Far from looking dull, the pergola creates areas of light and shade as well as changing the view to the rest of the garden, and its form can be attractive and intriguing. Add a bench or comfy outdoor chair and a large container, with or without a plant, and the picture is complete. In a smaller space, an arch can fulfill a similar role.

Decorative structures

All decorative garden structures add height and provide interest as well as the opportunity for additional planting space. Many also double as seating areas.

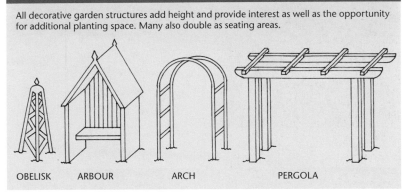

OBELISK   ARBOUR   ARCH   PERGOLA

Water

Constructing anything larger than a bubble fountain can be a bit of an undertaking initially, but once in place most water features require very little maintenance, and the benefits will be immeasurable. Even the smallest body of water provides a delightful focal point, while a larger one can create a complete ecosystem, attracting wildlife that will help you to control pests.

If your primary concern is low maintenance, make your pond or water feature as large as you can. A pond with a balance of plants and wildlife will create a natural ecosystem that in time will more or less look after itself with just a little maintenance a couple of times a year, while a small body of water, such as a bubble fountain, is often more work, especially if it's in sun. Warmth and water encourage algal growth, which will cover pebbles and other damp surfaces. The only way to get rid of it is by scrubbing, which you may need to do several times over summer. If you have young children to consider, however, a small self-contained water feature is the safest bet; anything bigger

Even a tiny bubble fountain in a pot in a shady spot is enough to create a relaxing atmosphere.

should be securely fenced or fitted with a metal grid just below the water's surface to make it safe.

Water features

Moving water is endlessly intriguing, the gentle sound and the play of light enhancing the pleasure of relaxing in your garden. Pebble pools, bubble fountains and wall-mounted water spouts are readily available in a variety of styles, often in easy-to-install kit form. Some features use a solar-powered pump, others require electricity – and a qualified electrician.

Still, reflective water also adds a special dimension, and it doesn't need to be a large expanse. A narrow rill, which is fairly simple to construct and maintain, is a stylish feature, especially set into paving in a formal or contemporary garden. Wooden tubs or half-barrels are also popular.

Ponds

Although it requires some digging work, creating a basic pond does not have to be complicated, but it is important to take great care at the planning stage, because once the water is in place mistakes will be hard to rectify.

Planning and design

You'll find it much easier to site and build a pond if you opt for a shape

This neat, contemporary-style water feature contains the lovely *Anemopsis californica*, a plant that likes to be in a permanently damp site.

with curves rather than right-angled corners. However, if your garden is strongly structured with leanings towards formality or minimalism, or if the pond is to be above ground level, a geometric shape is better.

Ideally, your pond should be at least 60cm (2ft) deep. This enables a healthy ecosystem to develop, means the pond is less likely to dry up or freeze, and makes it possible for you to grow deep-water plants, such as the larger water lilies. In a wildlife pond, a combination of deep and very shallow areas is essential (*see* pages 56–7).

In a natural pond, with its own ecosystem, there is no need for pumps or filters. In a more formal pond, perhaps with goldfish, a

Don't forget

Never smash the ice on a frozen pond. This could shatter a preformed plastic shell and will certainly upset any inhabitants. Float a large rubber ball or piece of wood on the surface to ensure an area remains unfrozen. Alternatively, use an electric pond heater to prevent freezing.

pump can be useful for aerating the water and introducing gentle movement. Filters can also be beneficial to keep the water clean.

Pond maintenance

Most pond plants do not need feeding, but water lilies will benefit from a sachet of special water lily fertilizer in spring. This is also the time to divide and repot any plants that need it.

Blanket weed can be a problem in warm weather, particularly in late spring, but is easily removed. Use a net or a stick – insert the stick, twizzle it and pull the weed out. Place the weed on the side of the pond for a day or two so that any creatures can make their way back into the water.

In late summer, cut back any overgrown water plants. In autumn, cover the pond with a net to capture any tree leaves, or fish them out with a net on a regular basis. Left in the water, they introduce high levels of nutrients. As plants die down, remove dead foliage and put it on the compost heap.

Surrounded by plants in large pots, this simple, narrow water feature contains just a few plants to maintain the sense of formality.

Bog gardens

A bog garden is a permanently wet or damp area of the garden, sometimes (but not always) set alongside a pond. It is ideal for growing moisture-loving plants, which are colourful in spring and summer and are attractive to wildlife; amphibians love the damp shelter it provides. Select plants that are happy to have their feet standing in water. Most marginal pond plants will thrive in this situation, as will moisture-loving perennials, such as hostas and candelabra primulas (*see* right). (*See also* pages 57 and 61.)

Planting

There's a huge range of lovely water plants. For a formal pool, it's hard to beat water lilies, which prefer still water. There is a range of sizes, from the 'pygmy' types to very large ones. *Nymphaea tetragona*, with white flowers, is the tiniest, needing only 25–30cm (10–12in) of water. Golden club (*Orontium aquaticum*) has long, yellow-tipped white spikes of tiny flowers and makes a good clump in deeper water, while water forget-me-not (*Myosotis scorpioides*) will spread around the margins and has blue flowers from mid-spring to late summer. Include oxygenators and floating plants, too (*see* page 71).

Beds and borders

There is no doubt about it, plant care is the most time-consuming aspect of gardening. However, a garden is not a garden if it has no plants, so gardeners must accept that a certain amount of time has to be devoted to their well being. The good news is that there are many plants that perform well without too much mollycoddling and there are also ways to grow plants that don't involve too much work.

Rethink your plants

First, think generally about the way you garden. If you always seem to be popping bulbs in pots into the garden, putting out and digging up tender perennials, such as dahlias, and raising hundreds of annual seedlings, stop. All this is a lot of work: you can get plenty of colour from carefully chosen permanent residents, many dahlias will survive over winter in the ground if given some protection, and for additional brightness you can buy a good selection of annuals growing in pots from your garden centre.

Choosing plants

■ Always choose well-behaved, high-performance, easy-care plants (see pages 64–91).

■ When buying plants, avoid those described as 'spreading' or 'vigorous'. These will nearly always cause problems at a later date.

■ Beware of gifts. If your neighbour hands you a potful of plants over the fence, have a sneaky look to see what they are doing in his or her garden. You might find the reason why your neighbour has so many to spare is that they are rampant spreaders.

■ If you do accept plants from others, don't plant them out straightaway. Allow a few weeks for weeds or other problems to materialize, otherwise you might be introducing more than just a plant to your garden.

■ If you're starting a new garden or flower bed, it might be worth spending a little extra and buying plants that are more mature, especially shrubs and trees. Larger plants fill most of their allotted space much more quickly, so avoiding the need for time-consuming infilling with other plants, or weeding bare ground between them. However, they will be more vulnerable to drought when first planted than smaller ones.

Take a dispassionate look at all the plants that are currently in your beds and borders and be prepared to get rid of any that don't perform particularly well or that need endless chivvying and care. Take out those that need supporting, regular division or cutting back in order to thrive and replace them with equally attractive plants that are self-supporting, go for years without division and die down fairly neatly in autumn. Only easy-to-grow, high-performance varieties deserve space in your new low-maintenance plot.

Large groups of easy-care plants, such as grasses, create plenty of impact, while also crowding out weeds.

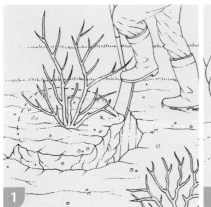

1

It is best to move shrubs in autumn or early spring. Using a sharp spade, dig a trench around the shrub in line with the outer limits of its branches and to a spade's depth.

2

Use the spade to undercut the rootball so the shrub is freed from the soil beneath; you may have to sever some roots. Slip a piece of thick polythene or cloth under the rootball (you may need two people).

3

Gather the corners of the sheet and transport the shrub to its new site. Plant it in a well-prepared hole, prune it to reduce the work the roots need to do while they are regrowing and water it well.

Less is more

Another way to cut down on the amount of time spent gardening is to reduce the variety of plants you grow. From a maintenance point of view, it is much easier and more efficient to have largish groups of the same plant rather than lots of different kinds, each with their own needs. Visually, this will also be very effective. Large groups of the same plant will have more impact and any individuals that aren't doing so well will be less obvious. If you also repeat these groups in several different parts of the garden you will achieve something that looks bold and self-assured and will distract attention from less successful areas.

Consider whether you can reduce the number of perennials you have in favour of growing one or two more shrubs, which are generally less work and fill more space in a shorter length of time.

Covering the ground

Bare soil grows weeds, so whatever else you do in your low-maintenance garden, cover the soil. You can do this with dense planting, which will choke out weeds. Don't overdo it though – check plant labels and allow a suitable amount of space for the plants to grow into, but avoid leaving huge spaces between them.

Another way to cover the soil is to spread weed-suppressing membrane (also known as landscaping fabric or geotextile) and then disguise this with a mulch of bark or gravel (*see also* pages 40–1 and 50–1). This method is useful when you're starting a flower bed from scratch, but has obvious drawbacks if there are already plants in place. It is

inadvisable to use gravel and other permanent mulches where you'll be digging regularly, since there is a lot of work involved in preventing these from getting covered with soil.

There are also plants that are called ground covers, for the simple reason that they spread far and wide, covering the ground. They are good in one way, in that they do suppress weeds, but the very fact that they spread easily means that they can sometimes become a nuisance.

White-flowered vinca is a pretty ground-cover plant that is useful for filling gaps and suppressing weed growth.

Raised beds

Raised beds are an excellent means of reducing work in the garden in a great number of ways (*see* box). They can be used for growing a wide range of flowers, even small trees and shrubs, and are also ideal for vegetables. Raised beds are fairly easy to make yourself (*see* pages 52–3), but to save time you can buy flat-packed raised beds at garden centres or online.

Designing a raised bed

Raised beds are very versatile. They can be positioned beside walls and fences or can be freestanding, and are made from a variety of materials, including bricks, stone, wooden planks (*see* page 53) or railway sleepers. Your choice depends on the style of your garden and the atmosphere you want to create. You can make them any shape you want, from rectangular to circular, sinuous or straight. Try to make them an integral part of the garden design.

Trellis or other supports can be attached to the edges of a raised bed to create further height. You could also incorporate a water feature, using either butyl liner or a preformed pool.

Consider having beds of varying heights, which will add to the visual interest. Several interlocking beds often look better than single ones scattered around the garden.

You can make a raised bed any length you like, but you do need to think carefully about its width and its height at the design stage, otherwise it could be difficult to tend your plants (for recommended measurements, *see* page 19).

10 reasons to install raised beds

1 If the soil is poor in your garden, raised beds allow you to introduce an area of good-quality soil where you can grow ornamental plants and vegetables with better results.

2 Gardening jobs such as planting, digging and weeding are easier as the soil is loose because it hasn't been walked on and become compacted.

3 Provided you've used a good-quality (preferably sterile) topsoil, you won't have to weed as often, because there shouldn't be any weed seeds in the soil.

4 The growing season is extended with raised beds as the soil warms up earlier than in ground-level borders.

5 You can adjust the height of the bed to make gardening more comfortable and less back-breaking – some like to garden standing up, others sitting down. This is particularly helpful for older or disabled gardeners. There are specialist raised beds available that accommodate a wheelchair underneath.

6 Raised beds allow you to garden where traditional borders wouldn't be possible or appropriate, for instance in courtyards, as well as on rooftops and large balconies (if they will bear the weight).

7 Raised beds are a simple and effective way to introduce changes of level, particularly in small, flat gardens, providing structural interest and making the space seem larger.

8 If used as a form of terracing, they are good for creating manageable growing spaces on steep slopes (*see* left).

9 Raised beds can double up as seating areas, so save space in small gardens.

10 Higher beds can be useful to screen eyesores such as compost heaps and recycling bins.

Don't forget

You'll need to water more often than you would borders at ground level. Small plants and vegetables in particular need watering during dry spells.

Terracing works in the same way as a spacious raised bed and provides a perfect solution for a sloping garden while adding visual interest.

Containers

Growing plants in containers is one of the most enjoyable aspects of gardening as well as the most consistently rewarding. You have so much control over the conditions they experience and can grow any number of plants that won't otherwise thrive in your garden. Pots can be used to enhance every part of your garden, but they are especially useful where plants cannot grow naturally, such as on patios, paths and steps.

Plants growing in the ground are always easier to look after than those in containers, so if you want a low-maintenance garden, keep pots to a minimum – perhaps just have a few large containers positioned near the house. The most important thing to remember is that you need to feed and water regularly, as container plants are dependent on you for everything.

Composts

When potting your plants, always use a fresh, sterile potting compost, never garden soil or home-made compost. The type of compost you use depends on the kinds of plants you're growing.

Large, permanent plants

For plants that are going to stay in their pots for a few years, such as shrubs and small trees, a loam-based (soil-based) compost (such as John Innes No. 2) is often the best choice. Loam-based composts retain

Growing a range of plants in pots creates a lovely display that can be altered with the seasons. Another bonus is that the containers can be moved around if desired.

nutrients well, so giving the plants something substantial to live on. It's a good idea to mix this with loamless (soilless) compost, which makes the growing medium more water-retentive, prevents it from baking hard when dry, and helps to keep it aerated. Loamless compost is also considerably lighter than loam,

Don't forget

Trees and shrubs will need root pruning or potting up into larger pots every few years, so don't put them into a pot with a rim that is narrower than its base, since you will have to break the pot to get the plant out.

Rhododendrons need acid soil, but they can be grown anywhere in a pot of ericaceous (lime-free) compost.

This blue fescue looks perfect in a tall, narrow pot and will never get so large that it becomes top-heavy.

which means that larger pots can be moved around more easily.

If you have an acid-loving plant, for instance a camellia, pieris or rhododendron, you'll need to use ericaceous compost, which is made without lime.

Smaller plants

Smaller short-lived plants, including annuals and many bulbs, do very well in loamless compost (such as

Bulbs in pots are traditionally given a gravel mulch, which looks neat and reduces water evaporation.

multipurpose compost). However, for smallish, long-term residents, for instance heucheras or sedums, it is advisable to add about one half to one third loam, because this gives the plants a little more to root into and live on.

Choosing a pot

Always try to match the size of your plant with the size of your pot. A large plant in a small pot will need constant feeding and watering and will suffer from the lack of root-run. It may also be in danger of toppling over because it may be top-heavy. At the other end of the scale, a plant that is always going to be quite small will not thrive – and will look insignificant – in a large pot.

The material a pot is made from will affect the growing conditions within it and, in turn, have a bearing on how frequently you have to water. Whatever style of pot you choose, make sure that containers are frost proof if they're going to stay outside all year round and that they have one or more drainage holes at the base to prevent waterlogging.

Terracotta Pots made from terracotta dry out fairly quickly, so if you use terracotta in a sunny spot, grow plants that are drought-

tolerant. If you have a shady spot, this effect is less marked.

Glazed clay Staying cool and damp longer than terracotta, glazed pots are ideal for plants that like moisture or if you cannot water frequently. They will stay damp for a long time in the shade, so check before watering since you don't want to drown your plants.

Plastic and fibreglass Pots made from plastic and fibreglass stay damp for a reasonable length of time but can get hot. They are also lightweight, which means they're easy to move but they need a sheltered site or will get blown over.

Metal Most metal containers will get quite hot very quickly in the sunshine, but work well in the shade.

Stone Natural materials, such as stone, tend to be heavy but don't dry out too quickly, making them ideal for permanent plantings.

Don't forget

Always position your pots where they will be in easy reach of a watering can and remember the smaller the container, the more often you'll have to water the plants.

Give plants a boost

If you want to get the best from your container plants, it is advisable to use water-retaining crystals and slow-release fertilizer pellets. Mix a scoop of water-retaining crystals in with the compost when potting your plants, and when you add water they expand into a jelly that slowly releases water back into the compost. The fertilizer pellets are pushed into the surface of the compost where they gradually break down, feeding the plant as they do so.

Plant care and maintenance

No matter how well you organize your garden, there is always going to be some work to be done. However, it doesn't have to be a slog and nor do you have to keep on doing it year after year. You can avoid quite a bit of repetition by doing a good job in the first place. If you share your gardening with someone else, divide up the boring tasks as well as the fun ones.

Soil preparation

Good soil preparation makes a huge difference to the health of your garden plants, leaving you free later on to sit back and enjoy the fruits of your labour.

Many gardeners dig organic matter into established beds and borders, but for weekend gardeners with limited time it makes good sense to dig over the soil really thoroughly in the first instance, when creating a new bed, and to adopt a no-dig approach for the rest of the time. There really is no need to dig if your borders are already full of plants that are growing healthily and happily, and there are those who believe that less soil disturbance is better for both plants and other garden dwellers. All you need to do is mulch your beds with a layer of organic matter each year and let the worms do the rest (*see* page 38).

Don't forget

Avoid walking on the soil in beds and borders. Your weight will compact the soil, reducing aeration and drainage. This is vital if you're using the no-dig approach, so you may need to introduce stepping stones.

Mulching

Mulching involves putting a layer of organic or inorganic material around plants. It is incredibly useful in the weekend garden, reducing the need for watering and weeding and improving the appearance of your borders. Both inorganic and organic mulches suppress weed growth and help to retain moisture, while organic mulches also improve the texture and fertility of the soil, stimulating plant growth.

Apply humus-rich organic mulch annually to your borders in spring or autumn (*see* page 38), and top it up around individual trees, shrubs, roses and hardy perennials at the same time and after planting.

The first (and only) dig

If you're creating a new border, preparing beds for the vegetable garden or if your soil has been badly neglected, thorough digging is necessary. If you're going to adopt the no-dig approach you'll want to do this only once, so it's essential you do it properly.

Digging is best carried out in autumn or early winter for most soils, but it can be done in spring, particularly if your soil is light. The most effective method is known as single digging, which involves making trenches across the border, filling the base with humus and then covering it with soil produced by digging the next trench. Make sure you don't dig so deep that you reach infertile chalk, sand or clay subsoil.

Add plenty of organic matter to your borders in spring or autumn, after weeding or when planting.

Most humus material is rotted plant material and will contain seeds. It pays to know something about it before you import it into your garden – go and check it at its source (such as the local riding stables or farm). Don't be lax about this, since you could easily be importing pernicious weeds. Before spreading it on your garden, check particularly for any long white roots, as these nearly always indicate weeds that are difficult to get rid of such as bindweed, couch grass, ground elder or enchanter's nightshade.

Adding organic matter

After the first dig, and every year thereafter, add a surface layer of mulch, 5–8cm (2–3in) thick, in the form of well-rotted compost, farmyard manure, composted bark and so on. This will improve soil fertility and structure and reduce weeds as well as the need for watering. There is no need to dig it in, as worms and other small garden organisms will mix it into the soil over time.

Mulching is best carried out when the soil is moist and fairly warm, in autumn or spring. If you're going to use the bed for sowing seed in spring it might be best to apply it in autumn; if you're going to plant out bedding in late spring or early summer it might be best to mulch in mid-spring. Before you start, remove all weeds and stones and prick over the surface of the soil with a fork.

Planting

Careful planting enables plants to establish quickly and easily and gives them the best possible chance of a long, healthy, carefree life. With a recently dug and empty bed, you might well be impatient to get the planting done, but it's better to wait for a week or two to give the soil a chance to settle and allow you to hoick out any weeds that regrow or germinate. This is particularly important with perennial weeds, which are very difficult to eradicate from planted beds (*see* page 41).

Planting up new borders

Before planting a border, or section of a border, water all potted plants well at least an hour earlier. If you're using a weedproof membrane (*see* pages 40–1), now is the time to put it in place. Arrange the plants still in

To help planting go smoothly, and make sure everything fits and looks good together, set all your new plants out in their appointed positions before you dig the holes.

If you're planting individual specimens into a bed already filled with plants, dig the hole at least twice as wide and deep as the pot and add some organic material to the base, along with some general-purpose fertilizer. This private food supply provides the plant with the nourishment it needs to settle in among all the competition.

It's very tempting to cram plants in, but don't do this, particularly with shrubs, as it will lead to trimming back and removing overgrown specimens later on. Always read plant labels to check the height and spread.

plant a shrub

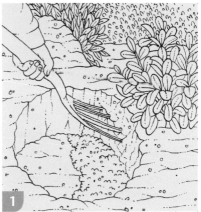

1 Dig a hole about four times the width and twice the depth of the rootball. Loosen the soil around the sides and base to make it easier for roots to penetrate. Mix compost and slow-release fertilizer into the soil removed from the hole.

2 Put some of the enriched excavated soil back into the hole and place the shrub in the centre, adjusting until the top of the rootball is level with the top of the hole. Tease out the roots a little. Backfill with soil, firm the plant in and water well.

their pots, adjusting their positions to ensure that each gets a look in and has enough space to grow into. Plant labels often provide information about eventual height and spread, which usually means about two to three years for perennials and five or more for shrubs and trees.

Dig a good-sized hole for each plant, so that it will sit with the top of the rootball just beneath the surface of the soil. (If you're planting through fabric, you need to make cross-shaped cuts in this first, *see* step 3, page 51.) Mix some general-purpose fertilizer, such as blood, fish and bone, into the pile of soil you've removed from the hole, then put some of this fertilized soil back into the base of the hole. Put the plant in place, backfill with the soil/fertilizer mix, and firm it in with your hands or a foot. Water well and then mulch around the plants (*see* page 37).

Supporting

The most important things about supporting plants are: get it done on time and do it properly. Waiting until something collapses under the weight of its blooms is just not sensible, since at that point any support will be very visible and stems and flowers may have been damaged. Also, emergency repairs

often have to be done at the least convenient time, which is not what you want if you can get out into the garden only at weekends.

Trees

Newly planted trees need to be staked for the first year or two, in order to allow the roots to establish and to prevent the top-growth from moving around a lot in the wind, which can cause damage. For pot-grown trees, put the stake in at a 45-degree angle to the ground (*see* below left); bare-root trees are best supported with a vertical stake.

Climbers

You automatically have to put up supports for climbers when you plant them, but make sure these are permanent and suitable. Leaving a clematis on just the bamboo cane it

Climbers look and grow better when they are properly supported; tie the main stems to the trellis.

Add a stake after planting a tree. Angle it at 45 degrees, with the top facing in the direction of the prevailing wind.

came with is not sufficient. Trellis, arches, sturdy obelisks and wires firmly attached to walls are all fine, and tying in new growth to one of these makes a very pleasant and rewarding weekend job.

Perennials

The perennials listed in the directory (*see* pages 81–5) should not need supports, but occasionally plants do grow taller and weaker than they should (usually due to not enough light or too much food) and then need some help staying upright.

Use a combination of twiggy sticks and garden twine, or buy a ready-made plant support (*see* below). It should provide a firm support about halfway up the grown plant, but put it in place in spring and allow the plant to grow through it, to hide it as far as possible.

Ready-made supports are useful for ensuring tall plants do not flop over when they flower.

Winter protection

For the weekend gardener, it's best to avoid plants that require winter protection as they're more work. However, if you really do want to grow plants that aren't fully hardy, put winter protection in place from the middle of autumn.

Tuberous plants

With tuberous plants, such as dahlias and cannas, wait until the first frosts blacken the stems, then remove these with secateurs. Pile a thick covering of organic material over the area containing the tubers. To keep the covering in place, drive short bamboo canes into the soil and slide a piece of chicken mesh over them. Check the mulch regularly and add more if very cold weather is forecast.

Container plants

Plants in pots often need a little help to overwinter safely. Move taller specimens against walls to prevent

them being blown over and group them together for a little protection against the cold. Tender plants that are too big to bring indoors must be carefully wrapped in bubble wrap or horticultural fleece (*see* below).

Controlling weeds

There are four main ways to keep weeds under control: good soil preparation (*see* pages 37–8); physical barriers (*see* below); routine weeding (*see* opposite); and, as a last resort, weedkillers (*see* box, below). It's best to try to keep on top of weeds, but you can never be rid of them all, so for your own peace of mind accept that your garden will never be weed-free and concentrate on doing everything you can to prevent their growth and keep the worst in check.

Physical barriers

In a bed solely intended for shrubs, climbers and trees, or one where you plan to create a scree or gravel garden (*see* pages 50–1), a covering of weedproof membrane (also known as landscaping fabric or

Using weedkillers

Most weedkillers are based on the chemical glyphosate, which kills all plants (including ornamentals) and is particularly useful for clearing very overgrown areas. It is considered relatively safe because it breaks down once it comes into contact with the soil. However, you must follow the instructions carefully.

Bubble wrap comes in handy for protecting frost-susceptible pots over the winter.

geotextile) can be a good way to keep weeds at bay. It will even suppress some weeds: as long as they're covered and deprived of light, they won't grow. Plants such as bindweed, brambles and so on will not be deterred, however, and should be removed beforehand.

Lay the weedproof membrane over the prepared, raked soil, then make cross-shaped cuts in the fabric so you can plant through it into the soil beneath (*see* step 3, page 51). Once the plants are in place, cover the fabric with a layer of mulch about 8cm (3in) thick; this will both hold down and hide the fabric.

As well as disguising weedproof membrane, mulches are also used on their own to reduce weed growth.

Routine weeding

If you've prepared your beds thoroughly, and perhaps used a weed-control mulch, there is not much to maintenance weeding and it makes a reasonably pleasant and satisfying weekend job. Use a small onion hoe, hand fork or similar tool to scratch out annual and most perennial weeds as they appear; annual weeds need to be removed before they produce seed, and with perennials you should remove the whole plant, including the roots. As the plants grow up and cover the soil, weeding becomes less necessary, since weeds won't be able to grow as easily in the shade.

Weeds to watch out for

Perennial weeds (top row) are very persistent and need to be removed completely, roots and all. Annual weeds (bottom row) are less pernicious but should be removed before they set seed.

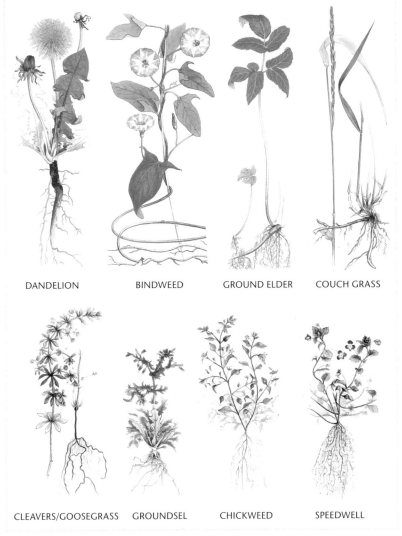

DANDELION   BINDWEED   GROUND ELDER   COUCH GRASS

CLEAVERS/GOOSEGRASS   GROUNDSEL   CHICKWEED   SPEEDWELL

Persistent perennial weeds are more of a problem and, if they take hold, may necessitate renovation of whole areas of your borders. Before planting a border, bindweed, ground elder, dandelions, couch grass and so on must be dealt with thoroughly. If they appear after planting, remove as much as you can of the growth and return to the task every weekend for as long as they keep reappearing. A quicker alternative is to paint the leaves with glyphosate, but even this will require several goes.

Watering

All gardeners should try to keep watering to a minimum by planting well, mulching thoroughly and choosing plants that thrive in the conditions in the garden. Plant in autumn if possible, since this gives plants a chance to get established during a period when there should be plenty of rain. Otherwise, all newly planted specimens will need regular watering. For most plants, watering every couple of days or so for the first two weeks is sufficient, unless the weather is very dry. However, for shrubs and trees it is well worth watering at least once a week throughout the first growing season, except when plenty of rain has fallen.

Once your plants are growing steadily, you can assume that they have developed a decent root system and should be able to survive without further watering. Drying out is more of a problem with containers (*see* pages 35–6), so it's worth limiting their numbers.

Feeding

The majority of trees, shrubs and perennials will be happy for a year with a good dose of well-rotted compost and a scattering of general-purpose fertilizer when they're planted. In subsequent years, it's well worth spreading a handful of slow-release fertilizer around them every spring and you can also give them a top-up of compost or farmyard manure. Some plants, such as clematis and roses, do need more food, however. It's important to get to know which ones these are in your garden, so you can give them what they need, otherwise they won't perform as expected.

Plants in pots rely entirely on you for all their food and water, so feeding them is much more important (*see* page 36).

Cutting back plants

Pruning and trimming are important for the health and appearance of a plant. However, you don't need to do it all that often and even most roses can be allowed to grow larger and more freely than is customarily thought. There are two main objectives: to remove dead and damaged stems and to keep plants shapely. If you've chosen your plants well, the second reason should rarely bother you. However, the first one is a fact of life: dead or damaged stems and branches must be removed in order to keep the plant looking good and to avoid further problems.

The aim of dead-heading is to promote further flowers and to keep the plant looking tidy.

Pruning

Trees and shrubs may well benefit from regular pruning, although many can be left to their own devices – it depends on the plant. When pruning, always make clean cuts using a sharp pair of secateurs, loppers or a hand saw, depending

Insert an up-ended plastic bottle with the bottom cut off into the soil beside a newly planted shrub. Water poured into it will be funnelled to the roots.

Use slow-release fertilizers, such as bonemeal, to feed established plants in the growing season. Sprinkle a handful or two around each plant.

Automatic watering systems

If you're unable to water as you're away, or if you live in an area with particularly low rainfall, you can install an automatic watering system. Available from DIY stores and garden centres, this allows you to set a watering rate and time. However, the disadvantage of such systems is that they will come on even if it's raining. Also, it can be a bit fiddly ensuring all parts of a flower bed receive similar amounts of water. The sorts designed to drip water into individual containers tend to be more useful.

Where to cut the stem

Where the plant has opposite buds, make a horizontal cut straight across the stem, just above a pair of buds. Where a plant has alternate buds, make a diagonal cut just above a bud. The cut should slope down behind the bud.

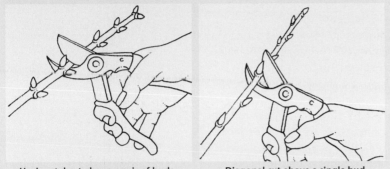

Horizontal cut above a pair of buds　　**Diagonal cut above a single bud**

Add a good variety of wet and dry plant materials to the compost heap; mix them all in thoroughly.

on the size of the branch in question. Cut just above a bud or leaf (*see* box, above). Once you've removed damaged areas, you may need to cut back or remove some other growth to rebalance the shape of the tree or shrub.

Trimming and dead-heading

A few herbaceous perennials look better for a quick tidy-up with secateurs after flowering; some, such as hardy geraniums, will grow fresh new foliage and possibly late-season flowers if cut to the ground.

Ground-cover plants need shearing back once a year to ensure they don't spread where they aren't wanted. Dig up parts that have grown out of their allotted space.

To reshape hedges, use a hedge

Don't forget

If you find you're endlessly pruning and trimming back you could remove some of those shrubs that repeatedly outgrow their space and allow others to grow larger and more freely.

cutter or pair of sharp shears. Most hedges benefit from an annual trim in the early autumn, but informal ones need be trimmed only when they are getting out of bounds. (*See also* pages 28–9.)

Annuals need regular dead-heading to look their best. Use your fingers or a sharp pair of scissors to remove dead flowers, including developing seeds. Clip old flower stems back to leafy growth.

Composting

Even a low-maintenance garden will produce waste green materials, such as dead and dying plants, weeds, grass cuttings and plant trimmings. With certain exceptions (*see* box, right) all these, as well as kitchen waste, can go onto the compost heap, where they will break down to create wonderful, well-rotted compost, which goes back into the soil and feeds the plants.

Compost is easy to make so long as you remember to mix it well. Combine dry and wet and bulky

and fine materials so none of them predominates. This will ensure that there is plenty of air in the mixture, too, which will enable healthy rotting to take place. For the busy gardener, a rotating compost bin can be a boon – it will save you having to turn the heap, and will ensure more even composting. You know you have good compost if it smells cool and damp and is soft and crumbly to touch.

Do not compost

- Perennial weeds (*see* page 41)
- Cooked meat or other cooked foods
- Cat or dog muck
- Diseased plants
- Thick, woody stems

Plant care calendar

This is a guide to the various jobs that may need doing in your garden and when. It looks like a lot, but don't worry – not all the jobs will apply to your garden or need doing every year, and some tasks are more crucial than others. Think about what really needs doing this year, make a plan that suits the time you have available and work gradually through it. Remember that timings vary considerably according to the weather and from one part of the country to another.

Some shrubs (like *Cornus*) respond well to being cut back hard and this also keeps them within bounds.

Early spring

■ Note areas that lack late-winter and early-spring colour and plant bulbs such as snowdrops and scillas.
■ Plan and start to implement any changes to the garden that will reduce maintenance in the future.
■ Plant pests, such as slugs, aphids and vine weevil, start to make their appearance from now on. Keep an eye out for them and take action as soon as you spot them: squash aphids and vine-weevil larvae and deter slugs with copper tape placed around pots and raised beds. You can also use biological controls.

Mid-spring

■ Sow vegetable seeds in the ground or in pots and plant herbs.
■ Plant perennials, shrubs and trees; add supports where necessary.

Slugs and snails are among the most destructive garden pests. Pick them off plants when you see them.

■ Start sowing annual seeds for summer colour. This can be done until early summer.
■ Feed the lawn; start mowing and trim lawn edges; plan lawn refurbishment for autumn.
■ New lawns can be laid now, although autumn is often easier since damp weather means less watering work.
■ Feed existing plants with a granular general-purpose fertilizer, which you can just scatter on the soil around plants.
■ Weed where necessary, water if the soil is dry then mulch thickly.
■ Check tree stakes and remove them where trees are well established (usually two or three years after planting).

Late spring

■ Cut back shrubs that have already flowered if they're overgrowing their allotted space. Also, prune evergreen shrubs to improve shape and reduce their size.
■ Repot long-term potted plants, adding water-retaining crystals.

■ Top-dress container plants that are not being repotted, replacing the top 2.5cm (1in) of compost.
■ Add slow-release fertilizer pellets to all potted plants. Cover the compost surface with a decorative mulch, such as gravel.
■ Put perennial plant supports in place where necessary, before the plants are growing too strongly.
■ Sweep or pressure-wash the patio and paved paths, particularly if in the shade.
■ Clean decking and apply a coat of wood stain or preservative.
■ Set up automatic watering systems if needed.
■ Tidy up informal hedges (wait until early summer if they are spring-flowering). Prune conifer hedges if necessary.

Early summer

■ Water newly planted trees and shrubs throughout summer.
■ Water newly planted perennials until new growth is vigorous.
■ Start and continue a gradual maintenance plan for the whole garden: weed, water and mulch

individual areas. If done properly, you shouldn't need to revisit areas more than once a year.

■ Now is your last chance to put in perennial plant supports.

■ Prune shrubs as required as they finish flowering.

■ Prune informal flowering hedges.

Midsummer

■ Water container plants daily.

■ Dead-head roses and other flowers as regularly as possible.

■ Tie clematis and other climbers to supports before they tie themselves in knots.

As soon as they appear, remove weeds from between paving slabs to prevent the roots getting a firm hold.

Late summer

■ Prune hedges. If you only want to prune once, now or early autumn is the time to do it.

■ Divide and repot water lilies; cut back any pond plants that are spreading too far in the pond.

■ Make a note of plants that are struggling in your garden. These can be divided in autumn; alternatively, dispose of them now if they have never done well.

■ Prune and tidy summer-flowering shrubs once flowering has finished.

Pelargoniums benefit from regular dead-heading throughout their flowering season.

Early autumn

■ Cover the pond with netting or maintain a regular routine of clearing fallen leaves.

■ Refurbish neglected lawns; grass seed is best sown now or in spring; turf can be laid any time.

■ Weed gravel areas and top up gravel if necessary.

■ Remove seedheads from plants you don't want to self-seed.

■ Plant bare-root trees; any shrubs and perennials planted now will establish with less watering work than those planted in spring.

■ Prune fruit trees and shrubs, if necessary, for improved cropping next year.

Mid-autumn

■ Move pots to sheltered positions to protect them against autumn winds and winter cold.

■ Protect tender plants with mulches or fleece for the winter.

It is so easy to plant bulbs in autumn for a brilliant spring display. Use a gritty, free-draining bulb potting compost.

■ Check supports for climbing plants and fix or replace any that are in a state of disrepair or rotten.

■ Check tree stakes, loosening ties as necessary. Even where trees are pretty well established (a year or two since planting), leave stakes in place until spring, because autumn and winter can be windy.

■ Continue with your pruning and tidying jobs.

■ Repair paving or top up gravel.

Late autumn to late winter

■ Do any major digging work during dry weather throughout late autumn and into winter.

■ Add manure or other humus-rich material to the soil, unless you've done this in spring. If you're not planting until spring, cover the soil with weedproof membrane.

■ Dig up, divide and move plants as necessary.

■ Plant bulbs, such as daffodils and tulips, for a low-maintenance display in spring.

■ Set up bird-feeding stations and replenish supplies frequently. Bird baths are appreciated, even if you have a pond.

Weekend projects

The five simple projects on the following pages are each designed to be completed in a weekend, assuming you have the equipment ready before you start. Each project is self-contained, so that you can fit the ones you like into your existing garden. However, you could do a complete redesign of your plot and use all of them together in one garden. The plan opposite shows how they might fit together in a small garden of 8 x 10m (26 x 33ft). Although the garden is full of interest, all of the elements are low maintenance.

The projects

The weekend projects are organized in ascending order of difficulty, starting with the wildflower mini-meadow, which is really very simple to make. Individually, they will all reduce the amount of maintenance work you have to do in the garden as well as enhance its appearance. If you do all five, you will end up with an attractive, easy-care garden that is not only wildlife friendly, but also provides a variety of vegetables and herbs.

The 'journey' round the garden

In the plan shown opposite, the house doors open on to a raised paved terrace planted as a herb garden (see pages 54–5). Herbs are planted into gaps in the paving stones and in the crevices. The terrace is surrounded by a low lavender hedge, which creates a lovely, scented space to sit and relax.

Steps lead down to the lawn, where granite or sandstone setts act as a mowing edge (see page 23). To the left is a gravel bed filled with drought-tolerant plants (see pages 50–1).

Stepping stones lead from the lawn through waterside planting to a bench with a view over the wildlife pond (see pages 56–7). Plants to attract wildlife in and around the pond give this area a wilder, more natural feel and help to divide up the garden.

A gravel path with timber or steel edging winds past the 'beach', where boulders and pebbles flow into the gravel along with airy planting, which is good for wildlife and adds height, texture and movement. The beach leads to the wildflower mini-meadow (see pages 48–9), which is filled with native plants and provides a transition between the informal pool garden and the more formal area of the lawn and beyond. The path continues to the lawn, passing the compost bin and tool store, which are screened from the house by a trellis and climber. A mixed border provides additional colour.

A raised vegetable bed (see pages 52–3) provides space for cut-and-come again lettuces and other salad crops and leads directly back to the herb garden via some steps (see page 27).

Getting started

Whether you're going to do just one or all five projects, spend a little time planning where the different elements would work best in your garden. It's well worth measuring up your garden and doing a rough sketch (see pages 18–19). Before starting any of the projects, you'll need to mark out the site. The method you use depends on whether the sides are straight or curved (see box, below).

If you're making the paved herb garden or wildlife pond, you'll need some levelling pegs. These are simply wooden pegs that you knock into the ground and use with a spirit level to check the site is level. When laying paving, allow for a slight slope so water can drain away from the house.

Marking out the site

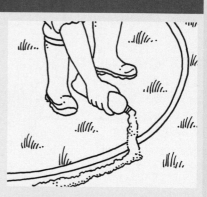

To mark out the perimeter of a proposed area with straight sides, use wooden pegs driven into the ground and string lines. Hammer nails into the tops of the corner pegs and secure the string to these, crossing the lines as shown. Check that the corner is a right angle using a builder's square.

For a free-form area, use a hosepipe or length of thick rope to mark out the curve. Try out various effects and spend some time getting the shape exactly as you want it – stand back and check it from a distance as well as close to. Use sand or builder's spray paint to indicate the shape.

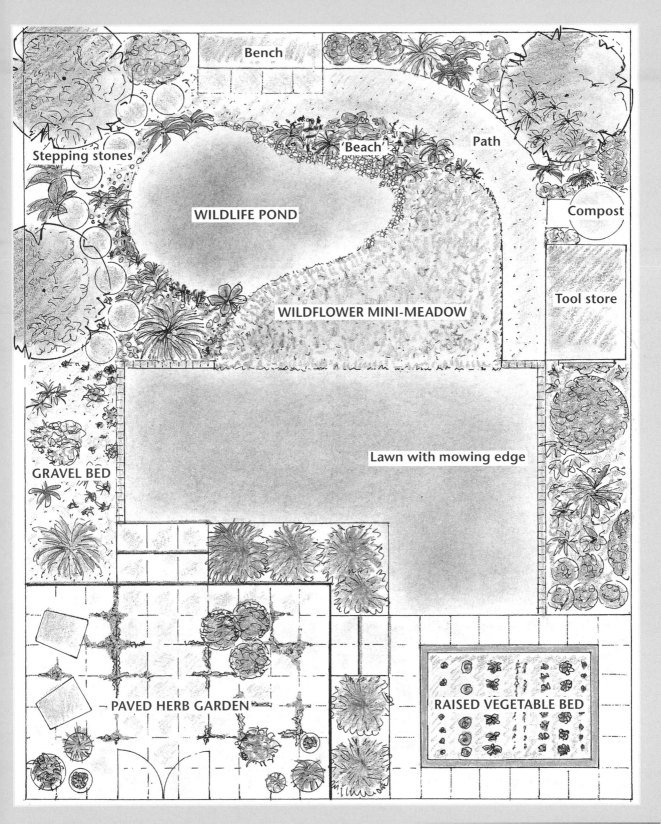

Bench

'Beach'

Path

Stepping stones

Compost

WILDLIFE POND

Tool store

WILDFLOWER MINI-MEADOW

Lawn with mowing edge

GRAVEL BED

PAVED HERB GARDEN

RAISED VEGETABLE BED

Wildflower mini-meadow

Planting a selection of native plants isn't just a pleasurable thing to do: our wildflowers and wildlife are threatened by human activities in the countryside, and making havens for them in our gardens has become almost essential for their survival. It really doesn't take long to set up the basic elements for a wildflower meadow – it makes a lovely feature for gardens of any size, and maintenance is minimal. However, you will need to cosset a tiny meadow more than you would a large one.

Snakeshead fritillaries prefer slightly damp soil and look wonderful in generous drifts with primroses and cowslips.

Planning the mini-meadow

The best spot to situate a wildflower mini-meadow is one that gets plenty of sun and is not boggy or overhung with other plants. Making it part of your existing lawn is a good idea, but don't have it close to the house, as rough-looking grass in this position will make the whole garden seem neglected.

The best time to make a meadow is late summer or early spring. This is because the conditions are most suitable for seed germination. There are three key steps involved: preparing the ground so the conditions are right, sowing the grass and wildflower seeds, and planting small wildflower plants.

Preparing the ground

Wildflower plants thrive in soil that is well drained and very low in nutrients. If you have a very neglected, starved lawn that has more weeds in it than grass, some of the work has been done for you. However, in most cases you'll need to remove the turf or, in a flower bed, the top few inches of topsoil, because this will be too rich.

You then need to dig over the soil as you would for a new lawn (*see* pages 22–3), but add a mixture of sand and grit or fine gravel to reduce the soil's fertility and increase drainage. If your soil is already fairly well drained, 2.5–5cm (1–2in) or so scattered over the surface will be sufficient. With damper soil add another 2.5cm (1in) of grit or fine gravel. If the soil is always very damp, choose plants that like moist soil (*see* box, opposite).

Ideally, you should now wait for a few weeks before sowing and planting. Weeds will regrow during this time, and they need removing with a hoe, a flame-gun or weedkiller containing glyphosate. This sounds drastic, but you don't want vigorous weeds competing with your wildflowers.

You will need

TOOLS
Spade, fork, rake, trowel, hoe or flame-gun

MATERIALS
Sharp sand, grit or fine gravel, silver sand, grass seed, wildflower seed, small wildflower plants, netting (if needed)

Contrasting sharply with a neatly mown lawn, this wildflower meadow plays a similar role to a traditional herbaceous border.

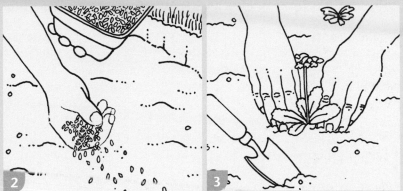

1 Mark out the site for the meadow, ideally making a natural, free-form shape (*see* page 46). If the soil is very rich, remove the topsoil or turf to a depth of 7–10cm (3–4in). Dig over the soil. Remove weed roots and other debris. Add a layer of sand and gravel (if necessary) and dig it in. Rake the surface again so it is level, then tread over it to settle the soil and rake gently one last time. Wait three weeks or so, removing weeds that regrow.

2 If the soil is dry, water it well with a sprinkler. Mix the grass seed with some silver sand so that you can see it on the soil, then scatter it very thinly. Sow a normal grass mix at about one fifth of the recommended rate stated on the packet. Next, sow drifts of wildflower seed. This will produce a more natural look and should help you to distinguish them from thuggish weeds. With a meadow mix, the application rate should be on the packet.

3 Next, plant wildflowers from small pots (these are sometimes known as plug plants). Dig holes just big enough to take the plug of soil, because you want to disturb the surface as little as possible, or more unwanted weed seeds will come to the surface. Water the plants before planting and water the planting hole. Finally, protect the meadow with netting until the seeds have germinated, otherwise birds may eat them.

Adding the plants

A wildflower meadow is usually made by sowing seed of fine grasses and wildflowers, followed by planting a few small wildflower plants that are difficult to raise from seed, for instance cowslip (*Primula veris*) and snakeshead fritillary (*Fritillaria meleagris*). Choose any grass mix that doesn't contain rye grass (you'll need to sow very thinly) and buy a selection of wildflower seeds. Alternatively, you can buy a special wildflower meadow mix. Base your choice on whether you would prefer a mainly spring-flowering meadow or a summer-flowering one. Spring flowers include lady's smock (*Cardamine pratensis*) and self-heal (*Prunella vulgaris*), while summer ones are often rather larger, such as ox-eye daisy (*Leucanthemum vulgare*) and greater knapweed (*Centaurea scabiosa*), though there are delicate varieties too.

Don't forget

Locally raised and harvested seed is best. Try not to buy seed from other countries, and never buy wild-gathered seed.

Aftercare

■ Remove unwanted weeds, such as nettles and thistles, as they appear.

■ Collect ripe seed from spring-flowering plants in midsummer; those from summer-flowering plants in late summer or early autumn. Sow them into a pot of loam-based compost immediately and plant them out when their roots fill an 8cm (3in) pot, either in autumn or spring.

■ Cut spring-flowering meadows in mid- or late summer and summer-flowering ones from early autumn. Use a strimmer, pair of shears or a scythe. Leave the clippings to dry for two or three days before removing them. After cutting, remove competitive species.

Suitable wildflowers

FOR A WELL-DRAINED MEADOW

Common knapweed (*Centaurea nigra*)

Wild carrot (*Daucus carota*)

Lady's bedstraw (*Galium verum*)

Meadow cranesbill (*Geranium pratense*)

Field scabious (*Knautia arvensis*)

Ox-eye daisy (*Leucanthemum vulgare*)

Hoary plantain (*Plantago media*)

Primrose (*Primula veris*)

Self-heal (*Prunella vulgaris*)

Germander speedwell (*Veronica chamaedrys*)

FOR A DAMP MEADOW

Bugle (*Ajuga reptans*)

Kingcup (*Caltha palustris*)

Meadowsweet (*Filipendula ulmaria*)

Snakeshead fritillary (*Fritillaria meleagris*)

Ragged robin (*Lychnis flos-cuculi*)

Grass of Parnassus (*Parnassia palustris*)

Meadow buttercup (*Ranunculus acris*)

Salad burnet (*Sanguisorba minor*)

Marsh woundwort (*Stachys palustris*)

Devil's-bit scabious (*Succisa pratensis*)

Gravel bed

Making a gravel bed is quick and easy and it will give your garden a clean, neat look within a matter of hours. From a practical point of view, gravel is considerably easier to maintain than a lawn or flower beds – there's no need for mowing, weeding is minimal as gravel suppresses weeds, and plants for gravel beds are usually drought-tolerant, which means no watering once established.

Planning the gravel bed

First, decide on the site of your gravel garden. Ideally, pick a sunny, well-drained spot. Although you want to aim for a naturalistic look, the easiest shape to make is a square or rectangle (*see* page 46); you can always blur the edges with plants or some larger stones to mask its formality. If your gravel bed is going to adjoin a lawn or a border, you'll need to add an edge, such as a wooden plank sunk into the ground, to keep the gravel in its allotted place.

Preparing the ground

Unless you already have poor, very free-draining soil, you'll need to make alterations, as shown opposite. This is because drought-tolerant plants often don't like too many nutrients.

If your soil is very heavy, it's worth removing the soil to a depth of about 15–20cm (6–8in) or more. Fork over the underlying soil, then fill the area with an imported mixture of 20 per cent potting compost and 80 per cent grit, coarse sand and crushed stone.

Using stones of different sizes adds visual interest without increasing the workload and creates an attractive background and contrast to the plants.

You will need

TOOLS
Spade, fork, rake, craft knife, trowel

MATERIALS
Sharp sand, crushed stone rubble, treated plank for edging (if needed), weedproof membrane, gravel of varying sizes, larger stones and boulders, drought-tolerant plants

Laying a weedproof membrane is usually recommended; it is permeable, allowing water to drain through while acting as a barrier for weeds. However, it's not essential. If you decide to do without, add a deeper layer of gravel to suppress weed growth.

Finally, spread gravel over the whole area. For a more interesting effect, include a variety of sizes of gravel, from small, pea-sized shingle to bigger pebbles and even boulders; you can use different colours, too. Arrange the boulders in a natural-looking way.

Silvery eryngiums, red heleniums and loose, flowing grasses create an informal display in this gravel garden.

Suitable plants

STRUCTURAL PLANTS

Cistus

Convolvulus cneorum

Cordyline australis

Eryngium giganteum

Euonymus fortunei

Hebe (smaller varieties)

Helianthemum

Lavandula angustifolia

Myrtus communis

Rosmarinus officinalis

Salvia officinalis

Santolina chamaecyparissus

FILLERS

Achillea

Artemisia 'Powis Castle'

Aurinia saxatilis

Catananche caerulea

Dianthus

Helenium

Oenothera speciosa 'Rosea'

Perovskia atriplicifolia

Potentilla fruticosa

Salvia guaranitica 'Black and Blue'

Stipa tenuissima

Teucrium fruticans

ANNUALS FOR COLOUR

Argyranthemum

Eschscholzia californica

Gazania

Lavatera trimestris

Limonium sinuatum

Linaria

Osteospermum

Papaver

Pelargonium ivy-leaved

Pelargonium scented-leaved

Verbena

Zinnia

Planting in gravel

In a gravel garden, unlike a traditional flower bed, you want space between the plants. Generally, fewer plants have a greater impact in a gravel garden. Avoid using plant supports if at all possible, to create a cleaner, more naturalistic effect.

Try to include a good mixture of taller, shrubby plants and grasses to provide structure as well as smaller, more low-growing plants to fill the gaps (*see* box, above). Annuals and biennials will provide wonderful splashes of colour in summer, and

Aftercare

■ Rake the gravel occasionally to keep it looking tidy.

■ Top up the gravel once everything has settled and every few years, if necessary.

■ Some of the plants will self-seed, so pull them out as required.

HOW TO make a gravel bed

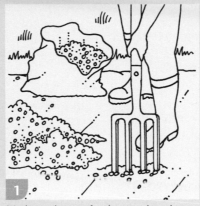

1 Mark out the area for the gravel garden (*see* page 46). Clear the area of all plants, including bulbs and roots. Dig the patch over thoroughly, remove the topsoil, and break up the subsoil using a fork. Mix the reserved topsoil with sand and crushed stone rubble to reduce fertility and improve drainage, and add the mix to the bed. Rake the site flat, remove large stones and other debris from the surface and walk over the soil to flatten it.

2 Spread the weedproof membrane over the area, holding it in place with large stones. To ensure all your new plants will fit and look good together, do a dry run by setting them in their positions before you dig the planting holes. The spacings will depend on the plants, but be guided by any plant care labels. Try to arrange the plants to look natural, such as in small groups with just two or three dotted out into the surrounding area.

3 Using a craft knife, cut crosses through the membrane to indicate each plant's position. To plant, fold back the flaps to expose the soil, make a planting hole using a trowel, insert the rootball so it is level with the soil, backfill the hole and, finally, put the flaps back into position around the plant's stems. Once the plants are all in place, water each thoroughly.

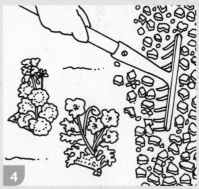

4 Spread a layer of gravel over the surface of the membrane and rake it so it is level, working from the edges to the middle of the bed. The layer should be a minimum of 5–8cm (2–3in) deep, to ensure the weedproof membrane is completely covered, to hold it down, and to prevent persistent perennial weeds from growing through the membrane.

there are plenty that are suitable for the poor soil found in a gravel bed. With some, such as California poppies (*Eschscholzia californica*) and field poppies (*Papaver rhoeas*), you can simply sow the seeds straight into the

gravel where you want them to flower, in early spring. For others, including zinnias and verbenas, a safer bet is to sow them in pots or seed trays under glass and plant them out when they're big enough.

Raised vegetable bed

Raised beds are a boon to the time-pressed gardener for a number of reasons: being nearer to waist level, they make gardening tasks considerably less arduous; the soil remains loose because it doesn't get trodden on, so digging and planting are easier; and there are fewer weeds, which means less work for you. If you want to grow vegetables but your garden soil is very light or heavy, raised beds are often the best way – you can fill them with the ideal growing medium and you'll get more crops for less space.

Nasturtiums are commonly grown with vegetables. They attract caterpillars away from crops and their flowers are edible.

Building the raised bed

Choose a level site for your raised bed and decide on its design, size, shape and position (*see* pages 19 and 34). Ideally, make the bed in autumn, so the soil will have enough time to settle over winter. If that's not possible, allow a minimum of two or three weeks between filling the bed and sowing seed or planting.

Always use wood that has been treated for outdoor use. Use planks of a decent size, about 40mm (1¾in) thick, because they have to hold a considerable weight of soil. A width of about 200mm (8in) is sensible, but you can make them wider if you wish.

The raised bed shown opposite is held together with posts, 50 x 50mm or 75 x 75mm (2 or 3in) square, at each corner. A long bed will need to have additional posts at intervals of about 1m (40in) to give it more strength to take the additional weight.

Filling the bed

Start by putting in a drainage layer of crushed stone rubble or gravel. Then, for the most effective growing conditions, you'll need to fill your bed with good-quality, sterilized topsoil and plenty of humus-rich material such as well-rotted compost or farmyard manure (half and half is ideal for vegetables). After sowing or planting, add a slow-release fertilizer to give the plants extra nutrients. As organic matter rots down during the course of

Vegetables often grow better in a raised bed because they like loose, fertile soil with few stones and have no competition from other plant roots or weeds.

EASY PLANTS
Courgettes
Garlic
Leeks
Runner beans
Salad leaves
Spring onions
Swiss chard

REQUIRE A BIT MORE EXPERIENCE
Beetroot
Broccoli (purple-sprouting)
Carrots
French beans
Peas
Radishes
Spinach

REQUIRE A SHELTERED SPOT
Aubergines
Chillies
Florence fennel
Peppers
Tomatoes

Aftercare

■ Water the vegetables often during dry spells and particularly after planting.

■ Weed regularly and watch out for pests and diseases.

■ Dig the bed over lightly each spring, top up the bed with fresh topsoil and compost in spring and autumn and cover the bed with mulch in autumn.

■ Your raised bed should last about six years, after which the soil nutrients will have been exhausted. Some of the planks may also need replacing, so take the opportunity for a complete refurbish.

the year, the soil level will sink. Each spring, you will need to add more to top up the beds.

Nearly all types of vegetables can be grown in a raised bed, but for the weekend gardener it's better to grow the easy ones, with just one or two of your favourites from the more challenging varieties. Choose baby or mini types and consider growing herbs and a few flowering annuals too.

HOW TO make a raised vegetable bed

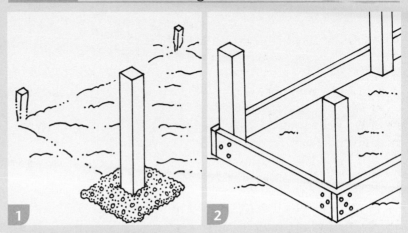

1 Mark out the area for the raised bed (*see* page 46). Use stakes to indicate the positions of the four corner posts. Dig a 30cm (12in) square hole for the first post. Put about 5cm (2in) of gravel or hardcore in the base of the hole, then stand the first post in the middle. Pour in a stiff concrete mix around it. Check the post is vertical using a spirit level. Repeat for the other posts, using a plank and spirit level to check the posts are the same height before adding the concrete. Leave it to set.

2 Start to build the sides of the raised bed. First, measure and cut the boards, allowing for the boards at the short ends to fit flush with the post and for the boards along the front and back of the structure to protrude beyond (as shown). Using a drill to make guide holes, attach the short board to the post with screws, then attach the longer board, fixing it at right angles to the end of the first board as well as to the post. Work your way around the remaining sides of the frame until the first layer is complete.

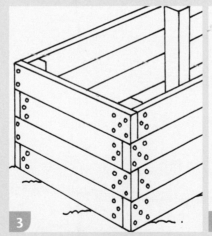

3 Build up further layers of planks in the same way, staggering the joints from one layer to the next (as shown) until you reach the desired height. As a rough guide, for a raised bed of 60–90cm (2–3ft), which is a good working height, you'll need three or four layers of boards, but you may need more or fewer than this, depending on the width of the boards and the height of the bed.

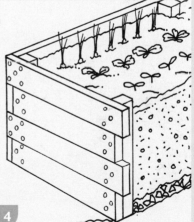

4 Loosen the soil at the base of the bed using a fork, then add a layer of crushed stone rubble or gravel for drainage. Make this layer approximately 5cm (2in) or more deep, depending on the height of the bed and how good your drainage is. Fill the bed with a mixture of topsoil and humus-rich material (half of each) and add some fertilizer. Plant the vegetables, water well and check for watering regularly.

Paved herb garden

A paved area will provide you with somewhere to sit and enjoy the rest of the garden and will reduce the amount of open ground, meaning you'll spend less time mowing, weeding and watering. However, large areas of solid paving can look uninviting and can lead to adjacent soil being damp because of water runoff. The ideal solution is to leave some parts of the patio unpaved. As well as being easier on the eye, this allows you to grow a range of attractive easy-care plants, such as herbs, in the empty spaces.

If you prefer to have a more uniform surface, you could lay the pavers with narrow gaps between them; these make the ideal spot for planting tiny thymes and Corsican mint.

Planning and laying paving

First, choose a level site for your paved area. If you don't want to cut pavers, measure your paving slabs, allow for a gap of 1cm (½in) between each one, and adjust the size of your proposed area accordingly.

If you want a patio for sitting and dining, allow a minimum of 2.5 x 1.5m (8 x 5ft) for two people and at least 3.5 x 3.5m (12 x 12ft) for six people at a round table. The area that contains the table and chairs needs to be wholly surfaced; restrict the missing pavers to places where people are not going to trip over them. Remember, it's well worth doing a paving plan (on paper or on the computer) in advance, as it's difficult to put mistakes right once the mortar has set.

Concrete or stone paving slabs are ideal. You can buy ready-to-use mixes for both the mortar and the pointing, which makes life much easier. For a successful result, thorough levelling and preparation of the site are essential. Before placing the pavers permanently, do a dry run by laying the pavers in position to check the fit and the look.

You will need

TOOLS
Spade, measuring tape, spirit level and plank, rake, plate compactor (from a hire shop), builder's trowel, wooden mallet or hammer, pointing tool or stick, gloves

MATERIALS
Levelling pegs, hardcore, mortar mix, paving slabs, grouting mix, planting medium of loam-based potting compost and sharp sand, gravel, herbs

Planting the herbs

Once you've laid your surface, it's easy to plant the gaps between the paving stones. There are many plants you can use, but herbs are particularly good, because most can cope with difficult growing conditions and few nutrients, and they are happy with sharp drainage and comparatively restricted root runs, too. Choose a range of

Don't forget

If you're building close to the house, you need to create a slight 'fall' in the surface of the paving to ensure water drains away from the house walls.

A mixture of spreading and upright herbs has been used in the gaps in this paving, but the path to the fennel-flanked bench is clear. The overall effect is very appealing.

HOW TO make a paved herb garden

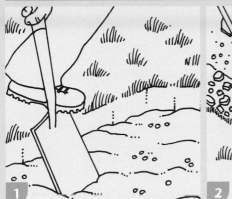

1

First, mark out the area to be paved (*see* page 46). Dig out the whole area to a depth of about 15–20cm (6–8in) below the intended surface level. If the paving butts right up to the wall of the house, the finished surface should be at least 15cm (6in) below the damp-proof course.

2

Knock some levelling pegs into the ground, using a plank and a spirit level to check that they are at the right height – about 10cm (4in) below your intended surface level. Then rake a layer of hardcore across the area. Use a plate compactor to firm it level with the pegs.

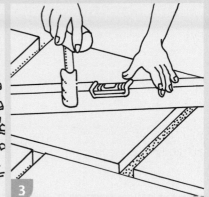

3

Using a builder's trowel, spread a small area of the compacted surface with a layer of mortar, about 5–6cm (2–2½in) deep; make the surface slightly ridged. Place the first paver in place, tap it down, then check it is level. Repeat for all pavers, leaving a 1cm (½in) gap for the grouting.

Suitable herbs

LOW-GROWING HERBS

Corsican mint (*Mentha requienii*)

Oregano (*Origanum amanum*)

Thyme (*Thymus*), particularly *T. doerfleri*, *T. herba-barona*, *T. leucotrichus*, *T. serpyllum*

TALLER HERBS

Chives (*Allium schoenoprasum*)

Tarragon (*Artemisia dracunculus*)

Fennel (*Foeniculum vulgare*)

Mint (*Mentha*) (many)

Marjoram (*Origanum vulgare*, *O. vulgare* 'Aureum')

Parsley (*Petroselinum crispum*)

low-growing herbs to put into the spaces in the middle and taller ones for around the edges (*see* box, above).

When planting between paving use a planting mixture that is half sharp sand and half loam-based potting compost. It is inadvisable to add soil from your garden, since this probably

4

Slightly dampen the grouting mix, then fill the joints between the paving slabs, pushing it in with a gloved hand. (Remember, you may want to leave some unfilled for more tiny herbs.) Finish the joints with a pointing tool or a rounded stick. Remove any surplus before it sets.

5

Remove some of the hardcore from the gaps, then fill the gaps with a potting compost and sand mix. Set each plant a bit deeper than the top of the rootball, then cover with more of the planting mixture. Finally, cover the soil surface with a gravel mulch for a neat and attractive finish.

contains weed seeds. Planting a little bit deeper than the top of the rootball prevents drying out and shrinkage of the light compost that potted plants are often grown in; reducing water loss is important, because although herbs are reasonably tough, they will find the environment quite difficult initially, until they get their roots down.

Don't forget

If you already have a patio that is fully surfaced, you could lift a few of the pavers and plant in the gaps in the same way.

Aftercare

■ Give the herbs a light, neatening trim once a year, in late summer or early autumn; use secateurs or shears.

■ Brush the paved surface occasionally.

■ Remove weeds between pavers using a patio weeder or old garden knife.

■ Use water and a stiff-bristled brush on light stains and dirt, if needed.

This project might seem ambitious, but follow a few basic rules, take it step by step and you'll see it's not too daunting. The rewards for you and for wildlife are beyond imagination. You'll be whiling your weekends away, marvelling at the creatures who have taken up residence, not to mention the visiting birds – and hedgehogs – who, conveniently, will feed on your garden pests.

Planning and making the pond

Ideally, make your pond in late winter. This allows time for the water to settle down and warm up before you add plants from late spring on. If you know someone with a pond, ask them to give you a bucket of water (free of pond weed) – the tiny creatures and organisms will be invaluable in getting your ecosystem off to a good start.

Choose an open, reasonably sunny site on level ground; avoid overhanging trees. The ideal spot faces southwest, with shrubby planting at one end providing shelter for wildlife. Decide on the size of your pond, bearing in mind that it should be in proportion to its surroundings. As a rule of thumb, a surface area of only 4 square metres (43 square feet) is enough to attract wildlife and give you room for a variety of plants. Leave space to walk all round it (it's easier for maintenance), and allow for a seat from which to pond watch.

A natural-looking pond needs a curving shape without sharp angles.

An amazing variety of creatures will arrive, as if from nowhere. As well as dragonflies, expect damselflies, pond skaters, water boatmen, pond snails, frogs and newts.

The golden rules for a wildlife pond are to include (a) shallow edges and (b) an area in the middle 60–90cm (2–3ft) deep. Shallow edges suit 'marginal' plants, and a long, gently sloping 'beach' with pebbles and flat stones enables birds to bathe, hedgehogs to drink, and frogs to come and go. The area of deep water should never freeze and allows tadpoles and other creatures to hide from birds. For a truly diverse wildlife habitat, you might like to add a bog garden at one end (*see* page 31).

You will need

TOOLS
Measuring tape, spade and/or mini-digger, spirit level and plank, craft knife, hosepipe, trowel

MATERIALS
Soft sand, felt underlay (or old carpet), waterproof butyl liner, edging (*see* opposite), pebbles, planting containers, aquatic soil, washed grit or gravel, plants

How much liner and underlay?
Width of liner: twice maximum depth + maximum width of pond + 30cm (12in) (for an overlap of 15cm/6in both sides)

Length of liner: twice maximum depth + maximum length of pond + 30cm (12in)

With richly varied planting and a diversity of wildlife and micro-organisms in and around the water, a pond like this will keep itself clean and make minimal demands on your time.

Making a wildlife pond

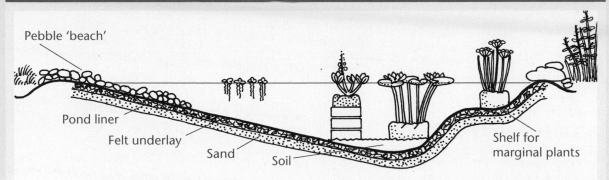

Pebble 'beach'

Pond liner

Felt underlay

Sand

Soil

Shelf for marginal plants

1 Mark out the shape of your pond (*see* page 46), then mark out a 15cm (6in) border all round for the edging.

2 Dig the hole for the pond by hand or using a mini-digger. Check repeatedly that the rim of the pond is level: place a spirit level on a plank laid across the pond's width and length. Reserve a small amount of soil to use later.

3 Make sloping sides, no steeper than 20° and even more gradual for the 'beach'. At the other end, 30cm (12in) below the pond rim, make a shelf 30cm (12in) wide for marginal plants. Continue digging, keeping the sides sloping gently.

4 Once the hole is dug, remove anything that could puncture the butyl liner. Spread 2.5cm (1in) of damp sand over the surface. Cover this with felt underlay, taking it over the rim.

5 Lay the butyl liner over the underlay so the middle touches the bottom. Gently ease it into the hole, over the planting shelf, making neat tucks as necessary along the sides. Do not trim the liner until you've filled the pond.

6 Shovel the reserved soil into the bottom of the hole.

7 To fill the pond, lay the hosepipe on the 'beach' slope and let the water trickle in slowly, so as not to disturb the soil.

8 To finish the pond, dig out the marked-out area beyond the rim to a depth of 15cm (6in). Trim the liner to fit, cover it with 10cm (4in) of soil and finish with your choice of edging (*see* below left). Arrange pebbles to form the 'beach'.

9 Plant into the containers using aquatic soil topped with grit or gravel (*see* below). Add them to the pond at the correct depths.

The depth of the hole you dig for the pond needs to be 8–10cm (3–4in) deeper than the final depth of water. This is to allow for the sand, underlay, liner and soil. Use a sheet of flexible butyl to line the pond.

Finally, consider how you're going to secure and conceal the edge of the liner. A mix of grass, plants, pebbles and flat stones will give the pond a natural look and benefit wildlife.

The planting

Pond plants perform a variety of functions – they shade the pond (which will help to prevent a build-up of algae), offer cover for wildlife and supply oxygen. Some have leaves that float on the surface, some like shallow

water ('marginals'), others like it deep. You need a good balance of species.

It's important to keep about half to two thirds of the water surface free of planting in order to let sunlight in and attract creatures such as dragonflies and damselflies, which need a mixture of open water and plants to breed.

Moisture-loving perennials and some marginal plants will thrive around the edges of the pond and attract wildlife.

For the pond itself, fabric planting containers are convenient as well as environmentally friendly. Anchor the plants in aquatic soil and top-dress with washed grit or gravel. Place each plant at the correct depth, as shown on the label. If necessary, stand containers on bricks, as illustrated above.

Suitable plants

SUBMERGED PLANTS (OXYGENATORS)
Curled pondweed (*Potamogeton crispus*)
Water soldier (*Stratiotes aloides*)

FLOATING-LEAVED PLANTS
Water lily (*Nymphaea*)
Fringed water lily (*Nymphoides peltata*)

MARGINAL PLANTS (EMERGENTS)
Water plantain (*Alisma plantago-aquatica*)
Flowering rush (*Butomus umbellatus*)
Water mint (*Mentha aquatica*)
Bog bean (*Meyanthes trifoliata*)
Water forget-me-not (*Myosotis scorpioides*)

Aftercare

■ Remove blanket weed as soon as it appears. *Never* use chemicals.

■ Expect some fluctuation in water level, but if it drops very low in a dry spell, top it up, using rainwater as far as possible.

■ Remove any excess of oxygenators in late summer, once the breeding season is over. Doing this in winter would upset hibernating creatures, and by early March you risk disturbing frogspawn.

(*See also* pages 30–1.)

Don't forget

Don't have goldfish. They don't mix well with native wildlife and tend to dig up pond plants.

Challenging sites

The most labour-intensive areas in any garden are those places where the conditions are less than perfect for the normal range of decorative plants. Getting a good display of healthy plants to grow in these spots can often take as much time as the rest of the garden put together. The best course of action is to go with the flow; there are a few steps you can take to improve conditions, but the most important thing is to choose plants that can survive naturally in these sites. Once you find plants that do well in your challenging spot, they'll soon become some of your favourites.

Dry, hot spots

In gardens the hottest, driest spots are usually beside sunny walls, fences or hedges. Very exposed areas can also be parched, especially where the soil is extremely shallow or where winds have a drying effect. Plenty of plants are adapted to cope with dry conditions, and choosing these for a dry garden will make summer maintenance considerably easier, as you won't need to water as often.

Improving conditions

Begin by making the conditions as good as possible for your plants by digging in plenty of compost or other humus-rich material. After planting, water well and then add a thick layer of mulch, as this will retain moisture (*see* pages 37–8). Gravel is an excellent choice for mulch in an exposed spot or beside a wall or fence; bark is preferable beneath a hedge as it looks more natural and will feed the hedge as it rots down.

If you want to go a step further, you could create a garden that suits the conditions perfectly. For example, in an open situation you could create a gravel garden or bed consisting of pebbles and stones (*see* opposite and pages 50–1). This sets the scene for a selection of plants that thrive in these conditions and look good in them. In a sheltered position, such as beside a wall, try growing more tender plants, such as succulents and those that look like they belong in hotter climes.

California poppies (*Eschscholzia californica*) have bright orange flowers for a long period over summer and flourish in hot, dry conditions.

Conditions are particularly difficult close to a hedge, because hedges take moisture from the soil. If you want to have plants growing at the base of the hedge, ideally plant approximately 1m (3ft) away, as the hedge's roots won't be so dense at this distance. You could even dig a trench and place a waterproof membrane vertically along it to prevent the roots encroaching into your flower beds. Alternatively, plant bright annuals in containers and place them in front of the hedge for seasonal colour.

Suitable plants

A gravel garden often works best with just a limited selection of plants, in particular those that self-seed gently into the gravel, such as California poppy (*Eschscholzia californica*) and dusty miller (*Lychnis coronaria*). Thrift (*Armeria maritima*) and Mount Etna broom (*Genista aetnensis*) will also thrive here. Succulents to grow beside a sunny wall include the tender *Aeonium arboreum* and Livingstone daisy (*Dorotheanthus bellidiformis*), or hardy sempervivums and sedums.

More plants for hot, dry sites

Allium	*Lavandula*
Artemisia (many)	*Osteospermum* (many)
Cistus × purpureus	*Perovskia atriplicifolia*
Colchicum	*Rosmarinus* (rosemary)
Crocus	
Erigeron karvinskianus	*Scilla*
Eryngium (many)	*Stachys byzantinus*
Gazania	*Thymus* (thyme)
Gladiolus	*Tulipa* species

Shady sites

If you have a shady spot with moist but well-drained soil, it's relatively easy to grow a considerable range of plants. More challenging are very dry or very wet sites in shade, although there's plenty you can do to improve both these, particularly if you're prepared to spend a little extra time on them. You could also make the area attractive without using plants, which is a good alternative for the busy weekend gardener.

Partial shade

There are plenty of plants to grow in places that are shaded for part of the day, such as beside evergreens and fences or walls. This type of situation is really only challenging if it is also particularly dry or wet, in which case adding plenty of humus will go a long way towards improving the conditions. Plants that love partial shade include ferns, euonymus, hellebores, alchemilla and brunnera.

Under deciduous trees and shrubs, there is little shade in winter but in summer the shade deepens and the soil becomes very dry. In this situation, it's easy to grow spring bulbs, including daffodils (*Narcissus*), snowdrops (*Galanthus*) and wood anemones (*Anemone nemorosa*), and forget-me-nots (*Myosotis*), but for summer flowers you'll need to grow plants at the edge of the shady area; hydrangeas are fine if the soil is reasonably damp, as are astrantias (*Astrantia major*), and there are plenty more. Ferns also do well here, whether the soil is dry or damp.

Permanent shade

Where the shade is more or less permanent, spotted laurel (*Aucuba japonica*) or low-growing evergreen cotoneasters, such as *Cotoneaster horizontalis* or *Cotoneaster dammeri*, are good choices, as are ivies (*Hedera*) and dead-nettles (*Lamium*), which really come into their own here. Don't dismiss all ivies as being rampant troublemakers – there are plenty that are very well behaved and suitable for a low-maintenance garden (*see* box, below).

In very deep shade, it's easiest to substitute plants with colourful sculptures, or perhaps a mirror to reflect some light. Where surrounding buildings are the cause of the shade, a small water feature standing on pale paving stones or light-coloured gravel is very effective in bringing life to a dark corner. If you must have colour, grow pots of flowering plants in the sunshine and move them into the shade for a couple of weeks of brilliant display.

Don't forget

Plants rarely grow right beside the trunks of mature trees, since the tree roots will always make life difficult. Instead, make a feature of the trunk – a bench built around it could look very attractive – and plant further out.

More plants for shade

Asplenium scolopendrium	Hedera helix (many)
Bergenia	Hedera hibernica
Dryopteris (many)	Heuchera
Epimedium	Liriope muscari
Geranium (many)	Polystichum (many)
Hedera algeriensis 'Ravensholst'	Pulmonaria
	Saxifraga
	Viola (most)

Surrounded by ferns, ivies and other shade-loving foliage plants, this quirky, stone water feature brightens a dark corner.

Damp sites

Provided there is some light, damp sites are only a problem if you're trying to grow things that don't like wet conditions. There are plenty of plants that are happy to have their feet in water or mud, and they're often fairly self-sufficient too. If light levels are extremely low, it's advisable not to grow plants but to use other forms of decoration in that part of your garden (*see* opposite).

Managing damp patches

A permanently damp patch, perhaps due to a high water table, is much easier to manage than one that is variably damp then dry, depending on the weather. If you were to plant such an area with moisture-loving plants, a dry spell could leave them in conditions they're unlikely to enjoy. So first and foremost, you need to ensure that moist soil will remain moist. There are two ways of doing this: if you're reasonably sure the soil will be damp for most of the time, the addition of a good load of humus should do the trick. However, if you think it could dry out, it pays to turn the ground into a proper bog garden (*see* page 31).

The tall, striking stems of *Primula pulverulenta* look wonderful emerging from the damp ground alongside a pond or stream.

More plants for damp situations

Ajuga reptans	Lysichiton americanus
Camassia leichtlinii	Molinia caerulea 'Variegata'
Iris sibirica	Osmunda regalis
Leucojum vernum	Pulmonaria
Ligularia dentata	Rodgersia (many)

Plants for damp ground

Large size seems to be common among bog plants, and among the most eye-catching and easy of plants for damp ground is the tall goat's beard (*Aruncus dioicus*), which has ferny foliage and white, frothy flowers. For smaller spaces, opt for the less majestic *Aruncus dioicus* 'Kneiffii', or choose astilbes, which are very similar and come in a range of colours. The yellow globe flower, *Trollius europaeus*, is also reasonably small and rather like a large buttercup, so is a good choice if you're after a natural look. There is a range of moisture-loving primulas, including *Primula vialii* and *Primula japonica*. If they like your conditions, they will spread without causing problems and produce a wonderful display in early summer.

Globe flower (*Trollius europaeus*) thrives in a damp spot, here with the upright leaves of *Iris pallida* 'Variegata'.

Tricky soils

The best way to achieve a successful easy-care garden is to grow plants that like your soil and avoid those that really do not. But what about those soils that present a challenge to even the most easy-going plants? Well, there are ways to improve some of the most difficult soils and increase the range of plants that can survive in them.

Sandy and clay soils

The ideal soil is loam, but most of us have loam with either some sand or some clay. The extremes are very sandy or very clayey. Sandy soil is low in nutrients and usually very free-draining, which makes it rather dry, while clay soil is full of nutrients but drains poorly, making it generally cold and wet, so although it's very fertile many plants find it difficult to grow in.

Most roses, such as 'Teasing Georgia', do well on clay soils. The heavy conditions don't bother them and they like the nutrients.

Improving growing conditions

Both sandy and clay soils can be improved dramatically by adding plenty of well-rotted farmyard manure or other humus-rich material. This provides the sand with moisture-retentive properties and nutrients, and it opens up the clay, reducing its stickiness and thus increasing the air supply to plant roots and improving drainage. This will need to be carried out each year, since the humus will eventually rot away to nothing.

Choosing the right plants

Once you have improved your soil, make the most of its underlying nature by picking plants that are likely to thrive in it. Roses are well known for loving clay soil (they enjoy the abundance of nutrients), while Mediterranean plants, such as lavender and cistus, revel in the sharp drainage that is characteristic of sand.

Free-draining sand is the perfect soil for most sedums, including the large, spectacular *Sedum* 'Herbstfreude'.

Don't forget

If the plants you want to grow won't thrive in your soil, you could use containers or build raised beds, where you have control of the growing medium (see pages 34 and 52–3).

More plants for sandy and clay soils

SANDY SOIL	CLAY SOIL
Brachyglottis Dunedin Group 'Sunshine'	*Ajuga reptans*
	Aster amellus
Cistus	*Aucuba japonica*
Cytisus	*Berberis*
Erodium	*Chaenomeles speciosa*
Erysimum	
Genista	*Choisya ternata*
Kniphofia	*Osmanthus*
Lupinus arboreus	*Philadelphus*
Lychnis coronaria	*Ribes sanguineum*
Potentilla	*Sambucus nigra*
Santolina chamaecyparissus	*Spiraea*
	Viburnum davidii
Sempervivum	*Viburnum opulus*

Verbascums will do well in most dryish conditions, but they are happiest in alkaline soils that are low in nutrients.

Acid and alkaline soils

The acidity or alkalinity of your soil will determine which plants will grow happily in your garden. It is assessed on a scale known as pH, with pH 1 being extremely acid and pH 14 being extremely alkaline. Most garden soils are much more moderate than either of these and are usually just above or just below pH 7, which is called neutral. However, it's well worth checking what sort of soil you have by using one of the easy-to-use kits available from garden centres. Test several different spots in your garden, since the pH may vary from one site to another.

Acid soil

Moderately acid to neutral soil (pH 6–7) is fine for most garden plants, and if your soil pH is around 5.5 there are still lots of very lovely plants you can grow, including many conifers (see box, left). However, if you have an extremely acid soil (with a pH of 5 or below), conditions are a lot more difficult for plants, as they may not be able to take up sufficient nutrients. Although you can add lime to raise the pH of the soil (as is often done on vegetable plots), this is a labour-intensive process and works only temporarily. For an easier life, if you have a very acidic soil it's better to grow plants in raised beds and pots.

Alkaline soil

Alkaline soil often presents problems because it is usually fairly chalky, and often shallow, dry and low in nutrients. Also, there are some very popular plants that don't like growing in it, including camellias and rhododendrons, and many blue-flowered hydrangeas will have pink flowers in soil with a high pH.

If you have an alkaline soil, It's best to choose plants that thrive in these conditions (see box, left). If you really want to grow lime-hating plants, put them in pots or raised beds filled with ericaceous compost.

More plants for acid and alkaline soils

ACID SOIL	ALKALINE SOIL
Calluna	Asplenium scolopendrium
Camellia	Bouteloua gracilis
Deschampsia flexuosa	Campanula lactiflora
Kalmia	Campanula latifolia
Kirengeshoma palmata	Erysimum
Liriope muscari	Helleborus niger
Lithodora diffusa 'Heavenly Blue'	Knautia macedonica
Molinia caerulea	Milium effusum 'Aureum'
Pieris	Pulsatilla vulgaris
Rhododendron	Scabiosa
Skimmia	Sisyrinchium
Vaccinium	

Many heathers and heaths are natives of damp acid moorland and can easily cope with acid garden soil. This is Erica carnea 'Myretoun Ruby'.

Recommended easy-care plants

The dazzling array of plants on display in garden centres can be incredibly tempting, but bear in mind that not all plants are suitable for the weekend gardener – some need cosseting to look their best, and many are beautiful for only a short time. This directory contains a wide range of high-performance plants that provide interest for many months of the year and have few, if any, behavioural problems. You can be confident that all will make a wonderful contribution to your garden – and are easy to care for.

About this directory

The following directory is divided into sections and features trees (pages 65–7), shrubs (68–76), roses (77–8), climbers and wall shrubs (79–80), perennials (81–5), ferns and grasses (86–7), bulbs (88–9), and annuals and other bedding (90–1).

Evergreen plants provide interest throughout the year, but some also have seasonal interest, for example if they flower or their leaves colour. When this is the case, the season of main interest (see key, below) indicates when they look their best.

All the plants featured are widely available. If you are bent on a garden that is easy to look after, stick to the plants mentioned here; varieties that have similar names may not be quite as reliable.

KEY to symbols

In this chapter the following symbols are used to indicate a plant's preferred growing conditions. A rough idea is also given as to what each plant's height (H) and spread (S) might be at maturity.

Unless otherwise specified, plants are fully hardy, deciduous and prefer well-drained, reasonably fertile soil that rarely dries out.

○   Prefers/tolerates an open, sunny site

◑   Prefers/tolerates some shade

●   Prefers/tolerates full shade

❄   Will survive winter in a sheltered site

❀   Always needs protection from frost

🌢   Prefers moist soil

◌   Prefers dry soil

pH↓   Prefers neutral to acidic soil

pH↑   Prefers neutral to alkaline soil

🍃   Needs humus-rich soil

❖   Season of main interest

Easy-care trees

Once established, trees are the ultimate easy-care plants and should be included in all but the tiniest of gardens. As well as adding height, they provide permanent structure and shade and screen unsightly views. They also encourage wildlife.

Acer griseum Paper-bark maple
○ ◑ ❖ YEAR-ROUND
H and S 10m (33ft)

The common name says it all: the main feature of this maple is its orange-brown bark, which peels away in thin, papery layers reminiscent of cinnamon quills. It also has spectacular autumn foliage in shades of orange, pink and red. Relatively slow growth makes it suitable for gardens of modest size. Shelter it from strong wind.

Acer palmatum 'Bloodgood'
Japanese maple
○ ◑ ❖ YEAR-ROUND
H and S 5m (16ft)

This small, oriental-looking tree is remarkable for its dark red-purple leaves, deeply cut into long 'fingers' that ripple in the breeze. Grow it in a sheltered spot, away from cold winds and late frosts, which can damage young foliage. Winged red fruits and autumn colour are bonuses, while its multi-stemmed form provides interest, even in winter.

Amelanchier × grandiflora 'Ballerina' Snowy mespilus
○ ◑ ❖ SPRING to AUTUMN
H 6m (20ft) S 8m (26ft)

Grow this lovely shrub-like tree for its long season of varied interest. The leaves open bronze-tinted in spring alongside delicate, starry white flowers. These are followed by fruits that ripen to purplish black, much loved by birds. The foliage changes from green in summer to red and then purple in a fiery autumn show.

Arbutus unedo 'Atlantic'
Strawberry tree
○ ❖ YEAR-ROUND
H 8m (26ft) S 7m (23ft)

Given a site out of cold winds, this evergreen tree makes a wonderful specimen, with its angular branches covered in red-brown, shredding bark. In autumn, clusters of small, pink-tinged white flowers open at the same time as ripening red fruits from the previous year. These resemble slightly warty strawberries but without the taste.

Betula nigra 'Heritage'
River birch
○ ◐ ◌ ❖ YEAR-ROUND
H 15m (50ft) **S** 12m (40ft)

Perfect for damp, or even quite wet situations, this easy, vigorous tree will also grow happily in drier conditions. Its main attraction is its gorgeous shaggy, flaking, cinnamon-orange bark, which is particularly noticeable in winter. Trees can be purchased with multiple trunks, to make the most of this feature. It has longish, yellow-brown catkins in early spring, and the leaves turn yellow before dropping in autumn.

Cotoneaster 'Hybridus Pendulus'
○ ◐ ◌ ❖ EARLY SUMMER to AUTUMN
H and **S** 2m (6ft)

This unusual evergreen thrives in sun (it will also grow in partial shade), where it will be swamped by tiny white flowers in early summer; these are followed by brilliant-red autumn berries. Its slightly wayward, weeping branches create a delightfully informal effect. Grown as a standard on a single stem, it makes a truly individual and very small specimen tree. Bees love the flowers.

Crataegus persimilis 'Prunifolia' Hawthorn
○ ◐ ❖ EARLY SUMMER to AUTUMN
H 8m (26ft) **S** 10m (33ft)

All hawthorns are attractive for much of the year, and this one is no exception. Glossy leaves, dense heads of white flowers followed by bright red fruits, and orange and red autumn colours – this tree has it all, including, please note, stout thorns. It is also virtually indestructible, making it an ideal choice for a city, coastal or windy garden.

Cupressus sempervirens
Mediterranean cypress
○ ◌ ❖ YEAR-ROUND
H 20m (65ft) **S** 1–6m (3–20ft)

Although eventually quite large, this dense, dark green conifer is narrow, making it suitable for most gardens. A reminder of Tuscan holidays, it forms an evergreen column, an eye-catching punctuation mark amid other trees and shrubs. Choose a position out of cold, drying winds, which can brown the foliage: this cypress is also known as the 'drama tree', because of its tendency to bend in the slightest of breezes.

Malus 'Evereste' Crab apple
○ ◐ ❖ LATE SPRING, AUTUMN
H 7m (23ft) **S** 6m (20ft)

Among the huge range of crab apples on the market, this has to be one of the very best. The first period of interest is in late spring, when masses of red buds open to white flowers in a breathtaking, tree-smothering display. The small crab apples develop throughout the summer, ripening to autumnal shades of orange, yellow and red. Pick them before the birds do, if you want to make jelly. The leaves are dark green.

Prunus cerasifera 'Spring Glow'
Cherry plum
○ ❖ EARLY SPRING to SUMMER
H 5m (16ft) **S** 4m (13ft)

Unlike many cherries, 'Spring Glow' makes a contribution to the garden in summer as well as spring, because of its attractive bronze-purple foliage, which remains this colour until the leaves fall in autumn. In spring, large, single, vivid pink flowers are produced in abundance on the bare branches. Its neat shape and short stature make this an ideal tree for small gardens.

Prunus 'Pandora'
Ornamental cherry
◯ ❖ EARLY SPRING, AUTUMN
H 10m (33ft) **S** 8m (26ft)

Ornamental cherries are grown mainly for their prolific, if not very long-lasting, displays of spring blossom. They are all lovely, and it can be difficult to decide which to choose. This is a very good one, with lots of dark pink buds that appear early, before the leaves, and open pale pink to white. When the leaves first unfurl they are bronze tinted but turn orange and red in autumn.

Pyrus calleryana 'Chanticleer'
◯ ❖ SPRING, AUTUMN
H 15m (50ft) **S** 6m (20ft)

This relative of the pear has a distinctive slender, conical outline with just a touch of formality and it makes a beautiful individual specimen in any garden. The branches are covered with plenty of lovely, eye-catching white blossom in spring, and small brown fruits follow in autumn. Surprisingly, these are shaped like little spheres rather than mini-pears. The glossy leaves turn red in autumn, hanging on until early winter.

Pyrus salicifolia 'Pendula'
Weeping silver-leaved pear
◯ ❖ SPRING to AUTUMN
H 5m (16ft) **S** 4m (13ft)

Creating a wonderful focal point in an informal setting, this tree has narrow, willow-like leaves that are particularly beautiful in spring, their silver colour fading to grey-green in summer. In addition, the slender, weeping branches are in charming disarray, rippling gently in the breeze. Resist the urge to prune, because this will spoil the informality; choose the similar *Pyrus salicifolia* and clip this if you want something neater.

Sorbus 'Autumn Spire'
◯ ◑ ❖ LATE SPRING to AUTUMN
H 4m (13ft) **S** 1.5 (5ft)

You don't need very much space to grow this small tree, which makes an upright and compact column; it is even worth trying it in a large container. White flowerheads appear in late spring, followed, later in the year, by heavy bunches of yellow berries. These look particularly good against the excellent autumn foliage in shades of red, orange and purple. Birds love the berries.

Sorbus hupehensis
'Pink Pagoda' Hubei rowan
◯ ◑ ❖ SPRING to AUTUMN
H 4m (13ft) **S** 3m (10ft)

Most rowans have lovely feathery leaves divided into many leaflets, and this is no exception. The almost oval leaflets are blue-green through spring and summer, turning brilliant orange-red in autumn. White spring flowers are followed by clusters of blush-pink berries. These fade to white, adding another element to the display and hanging on after leaf-fall – if they haven't all been eaten by the birds.

Taxus baccata 'Fastigiata Aureomarginata' Yew
◯ ◑ ● ◊ ❖ YEAR-ROUND
H 5m (16ft) **S** 2.5m (8ft)

This version of the common yew is about as columnar as a tree can get, with its straight-sided, pillar-like growth giving it architectural impact. The effect is enhanced by the gold edges on the needle-like evergreen leaves, brightening any dark corner – even if the colour is not so intense in the shade. Yews grow happily in deep shade and dry soil, making them very useful for conditions in which many other trees struggle.

Easy-care shrubs

Most shrubs require only minimal maintenance – just occasional feeding and cutting back (*see* pages 42–3) – and the ones included here are all particularly easy-going. They are useful for introducing a variety of heights, shapes, textures and colours into a garden. Choose a mixture of evergreen and deciduous kinds for year-round interest.

Abelia × *grandiflora* 'Kaleidoscope'
○ ◑ **pH↓** ❖ YEAR-ROUND
H 1m (40in) S 1.2m (4ft)

Aptly named, this compact evergreen shrub is a year-round performer. The glorious display begins in spring, with the appearance of new, bright yellow and green foliage. The leaves darken in summer, becoming deep green with creamy-gold margins, followed in autumn by a kaleidoscope of bold yellow, orange and red shades. Fragrant white flowers appear from midsummer to autumn and create a striking contrast with the reddish-purple stems.

Berberis darwinii 'Compacta'
○ ◑ ❖ SPRING and AUTUMN
H and S 1m (40in)

With its glossy little holly-like leaves, which have an attractive red tinge when young, this compact, evergreen berberis is an excellent choice for even the smallest garden. Rich-orange flowers create a vibrant display in spring, and are followed by blue berries in autumn. You might even see the occasional late flower alongside them, too, if the weather is mild.

Berberis thunbergii f. *atropurpurea* 'Rose Glow'
○ ◑ ❖ SPRING to AUTUMN
H 1m (40in) S 2.5m (8ft)

This showy shrub is grown for its brightly variegated foliage and it makes a good specimen plant as well as an excellent, prickly hedge. The leaves open red-purple, later developing a generous splashing of contrasting pink, cream, silver and white. Spring brings a good show of red-tinted, yellow flowers. Red berries ripen in autumn as the leaves also turn red and eventually fall.

Buddleja 'Blue Chip'
Butterfly bush
○ ❖ EARLY SUMMER to EARLY AUTUMN
H and S 60cm (24in)

This is the first truly dwarf buddleia. A well-behaved and unfussy performer for the smallest of gardens, it is also ideal for growing in a container. The pretty, blue flower spikes are completely in proportion with the plant and appear throughout summer, sometimes even into early autumn. They also have a delicious honey fragrance.

Buxus sempervirens 'Elegantissima' Common box
○ ◑ ❖ YEAR-ROUND
H and S 1.5m (5ft)

Box is the archetypal topiary and edging plant, its tight little evergreen leaves lending themselves perfectly to regular clipping. 'Elegantissima' is particularly dense in habit and has the added bonus of irregular, creamy-white margins to its narrow leaves for a much lighter overall effect. For the best-coloured foliage, grow it in light shade although, like all box, it will tolerate hot, dry conditions.

Camellia × williamsii 'Donation'
◐ pH ↓ 🍃 ❖ LATE WINTER to LATE SPRING
H 5m (16ft) S 2.5m (8ft)

With their very early flowers, camellias make a great addition to any garden with acid soil. 'Donation' is deservedly popular, with its glossy evergreen leaves and abundant large, semi-double pink flowers. Grow all camellias in a site sheltered from the early morning sun, which damages frosted buds and blooms. If you have alkaline soil, try them in large containers of ericaceous compost and water well.

Ceanothus × delileanus 'Gloire de Versailles' California lilac
○ ❖ MIDSUMMER to AUTUMN
H and S 1.5m (5ft)

Ceanothus are dense shrubs with powder-puff flowers usually in shades of blue (white or pink are also available). 'Gloire de Versailles' is fast-growing, with pale blue flowers relatively late in the year. Ceanothus are especially suitable for training on a warm, sheltered wall, where the plants can reach twice the height they would in an open site.

Chamaecyparis obtusa 'Nana Gracilis'
○ pH ↓ ❖ YEAR-ROUND
H 3m (10ft) S 6m (20ft)

Slow growth and a restrained conical shape make this evergreen, dwarf cypress ideal for a small garden. It has glossy, rich-green foliage in sculptural sprays that stick out in all directions, making it rather eye-catching, especially when young, and ideal as a focal point. It will tolerate chalky soils, but for best results in these conditions grow it in a tub of ericaceous compost.

Chamaecyparis pisifera 'Boulevard' Blue moss cypress
○ ● pH ↓ ❖ YEAR-ROUND
H 10m (33ft) S 5m (16ft)

Soft blue-green evergreen foliage creates an informal, silvery pyramid as the blue moss cypress grows very slowly to its ultimate height. As a youngster, it is a neat little plant that is perfect for creating vertical accents among less upright shrubs or for using as a focal point among low-growing plants, for example heather. It will tolerate alkaline conditions with plenty of moisture, but the foliage colour may be less crisp.

Choisya × dewitteana 'Aztec Pearl' Mexican orange blossom
○ ❖ LATE SPRING, LATE SUMMER to EARLY AUTUMN
H and S 2.5m (8ft)

All choisyas are good garden plants grown for their neat evergreen foliage, rounded shape and fragrant, star-like white flowers. 'Aztec Pearl' is particularly attractive, its narrow, linear leaves giving it a delicate, airy appearance. Its flowers have a pretty pink tint and appear in two flushes: in late spring and again from late summer into autumn.

Cistus Sun rose
○ ❄ ◇ ❖ SUMMER
H 0.5–2m (20–75in) S 1–2m (3–6ft)

Ideal for hot, dry situations, the aptly named sun roses are compact evergreen shrubs that produce a summer show of pretty, saucer-shaped flowers in white or shades of pink with contrasting yellow stamens and some with dark blotches. The blooms have delicate, papery petals and can be quite large. × obtusifolius 'Thrive' (white with dark green leaves) and × pulverulentus 'Sunset' (rose-pink with grey-green leaves, shown above) are low-growing, at 50–60cm (20–24in).

Convolvulus cneorum
○ ❈ ❖ LATE SPRING to SUMMER
H 60cm (24in) S 90cm (3ft)

Although not particularly fond of
freezing, wet weather, this lovely little
evergreen is reasonably tough and in
cold areas it can be grown in a container
and moved into a cool greenhouse or
conservatory for the winter. The silky,
silver-green leaves provide year-round
interest, and pretty, funnel-shaped,
white flowers open from contrasting
pink buds in late spring and summer.

Cornus alba 'Sibirica Variegata' Red-barked dogwood
○ ❖ YEAR-ROUND
H and S 2.5m (8ft)

This is a high-performance shrub that
has something to offer in every season.
Spring brings grey-green leaves with
splashy white variegation and creamy
flowerheads that carry through to early
summer and are followed by bluish-
white berries. The foliage colours
red before falling, but is completely
outshone by the thicket of stems: red
throughout the growing season, but
a glowing bright crimson in winter.

Cornus alternifolia 'Argentea'
Pagoda dogwood
○ ◐ ❖ SPRING to AUTUMN
H 3m (10ft) S 2.5m (8ft)

With its branches in floating silvery
layers, this dogwood deserves a special
position in the garden – somewhere
where the tiering effect can be fully
appreciated. Variegated leaves, fluffy
white flowerheads and little blue-black
fruits all add to its charm, but it is the
unique shape that really makes this
stand out from the crowd. It's not
difficult or fussy: simply plant and enjoy.

Cotoneaster atropurpureus 'Variegatus'
○ ❖ SPRING to AUTUMN
H 45cm (18in) S 90cm (3ft)

This diminutive cotoneaster has neat,
white-edged leaves that take on warm-
pink and red tints in autumn before
they drop. It has a scattering of small
red flowers in summer, followed by red
berries. The habit is low and spreading,
which makes it ideal for draping over
a wall or alongside steps, where the
delicate variegation of the leaves can
be seen up close.

Erica carnea 'Vivellii'
Winter heath
○ pH↓ ❖ MIDWINTER to MID-SPRING
H and S 30cm (12in)

Through the darkest days of the year,
this heath makes a bold statement, its
evergreen, needle-like leaves burnished
bronze by the cold, in contrast to the
massed ranks of purplish-pink flowers
that darken to a rich magenta as they
age. Its summer foliage is an unobtrusive
dark green. Plant it alongside other
acid-loving heaths and dwarf conifers
or put it in a pot for winter displays.

Erica × darleyensis f. albiflora 'White Perfection'
Darley dale heath
○ pH↓ ❖ EARLY WINTER to MID-SPRING
H 40cm (16in) S 70cm (28in)

A very dense carpet of bright evergreen
foliage and copious spikes of pure white
flowers, produced continuously from
early winter to mid-spring, make this
heath really good value. It is robust and
vigorous too, so makes ideal low-
maintenance ground cover on a bank
or anywhere where access for weeding
is tricky. Grow it with other heaths and
heathers, as well as dwarf conifers.

Euonymus fortunei 'Silver Queen'
◐ ◐ ❖ YEAR-ROUND
H 1.2m (4ft) S 1.5m (5ft)

One of the garden stalwarts, this is a reliable, weather-resistant evergreen that does well almost anywhere, even in poor soil. Its oval, bright cream-variegated leaves will light up a shady border, although they often colour best in full sun. A compact, bushy shrub, it can also be trained against a wall or even up a suitable tree, where it can eventually reach a height of 2.5m (8ft) or more.

Euonymus japonicus 'Bravo'
◐ ◐ ❖ YEAR-ROUND
H and S 50cm (20in)

A winning combination of low growth and relatively large, warm cream-variegated leaves make this an ideal evergreen for the smallest space. Grow it as a sturdy, bell-shaped shrub, perhaps in a container, or plant a row as an eye-catching edging to a larger bed or border. It tolerates trimming well, but take care not to cut through individual leaves since this will look very messy.

Euonymus japonicus 'Green Rocket'
◐ ◐ ❖ YEAR-ROUND
H 1m (40in) S 1.5m (5ft)

With its virtually indestructible constitution and neat little dark green leaves (sometimes with a yellow edge) arranged in whorls around distinctive upright stems, this small evergreen shrub is excellent for creating a low hedge. It is perfect for a breezy coastal garden, where a taller hedge might spoil the sea views, or it can be clipped tightly to fit into more formal settings.

Fuchsia 'Mrs Popple'
◐ ◐ ❄ ❖ SUMMER to AUTUMN
H and S 1m (40in)

One of just a few almost-hardy fuchsias (there are hundreds of the tender bedding types), this is a great shrub for a sheltered spot. It has brightly coloured, slender flowers in true fuchsia colours: violet-purple 'skirts' surrounded by dazzling scarlet 'tops'. In mild areas, 'Mrs Popple' makes a striking informal hedge, but it is probably at its best as an unclipped, freestanding shrub.

Griselinia littoralis 'Variegata'
Broadleaf
◡ ❄ ❖ YEAR-ROUND
H 3m (10ft) S 2m (6ft)

Evergreen and variegated, this is a lovely foliage shrub for an informal hedge or screen in milder gardens. The new leaves have gold edges that later fade to creamy white, creating a lively contrast with the bright apple-green centres. The variegation is prettily streaked and there are hints of grey-green too, so choose a position where the foliage can be seen close up.

Hebe
◐ ◐ ❖ YEAR-ROUND
H and S 30–150cm (1–5ft)

Hebes are neat, evergreen shrubs that are happy almost anywhere, so long as they have some sunshine and a little shelter from cold winds. Their leaves are in shades of pale blue-grey to dark green, and the smaller ones are often usefully dome-shaped, making lovely low focal points. For additional foliage interest try 'Caledonia' (green leaves suffused rose-purple in the cold; violet summer flowers) or 'Red Edge' (red-purple leaf margins; white flowers; shown above).

Helianthemum 'Rhodanthe Carneum' Rock rose

○ ❖ LATE SPRING to MIDSUMMER

H and S 30cm (12in)

Rock roses are perfect for breaking up the edge of paving or gravel, or for tumbling over the side of a raised bed. Flowering for a long period, they have narrow, evergreen leaves and a tidy habit. 'Rhodanthe Carneum' (formerly 'Wisley Pink') has pink blooms with a yellow centre and grey-green foliage. Other varieties include 'Fire Dragon' (orange-red), 'Wisley Primrose' (yellow) and 'Wisley White'.

Hydrangea arborescens 'Annabelle'

○ ◑ 🍃 ❖ SUMMER

H and S 2.5m (8ft)

This lovely hydrangea has an open habit and spherical white flowerheads consisting of many tiny florets – which make it rather softer in appearance than the traditional 'mophead' types. The flowerheads can be up to 30cm (12in) across, which gives the plant plenty of impact. It could do with a site that offers some shelter from late frosts and enjoys some support. Pruning keeps it smaller and more compact if need be.

Hydrangea paniculata 'Kyushu'

○ ◑ 🍃 ❖ LATE SUMMER to EARLY AUTUMN

H 5m (16ft) S 2.5m (8ft)

Producing airy cones of white flowers (with a hint of green when young), this shrub is truly something to behold when in bloom. It has an upright habit, which means it doesn't feel the need to spread outwards as far as some of the other hydrangeas – and it looks fine if just a little bit squashed. So choose this one if you need to fill an awkward gap in a woodland-style border.

Hydrangea serrata 'Bluebird'

○ ◑ ❄ 🍃 ❖ SUMMER to AUTUMN

H and S 1.2m (4ft)

'Bluebird' is a 'lacecap' hydrangea, so it has a combination of large sterile flowers and tiny fertile ones, arranged rather like delicate needlework. The blue colouring is at its richest on acid soil; on alkaline soil, the flowers are a less showy shade of pink-purple. This plant has a long flowering period, and red and orange autumn leaves, making it a wonderful all-rounder for a small, sheltered garden.

Juniperus × pfitzeriana 'Sulphur Spray'

○ ◑ ❖ YEAR-ROUND

H and S 1.5m (5ft)

This medium-sized juniper is a brilliant focal point, with its striking shape, created by graceful, ascending branches that eventually form a flat-topped bush of tiered foliage. The bright golden-yellow evergreen leaves fade to creamy green in winter and the small, round deep-blue berries become paler. Grow this plant as a contrast to more upright shrubs. It also looks wonderful where it can overhang a path or wall or, even better, reflected in a clear, still pond.

Juniperus squamata 'Blue Star' Flaky juniper

○ ◑ ❖ YEAR-ROUND

H 40cm (16in) S 1m (40in)

Not just squat but practically prostrate, this stubby little juniper has short, spreading branches that make excellent ground cover in a well-drained spot. Its silver-blue, evergreen foliage provides an ideal foil for more upright, green-leaved conifers, and it also looks good beside gravel or a paved patio, where its irregular shape comes into its own as a softening contrast for hard edges.

Lavandula angustifolia 'Hidcote' Lavender
○ ❖ MID- to LATE SUMMER
H 60cm (24in) S 75cm (30in)

Some traditional lavenders can become leggy and ragged within just a couple of years, but there are also a number of compact cultivars available. This is one such, and it has silvery-grey evergreen foliage and deep-purple flowers, both of which look especially good when grown *en masse* as edging. Trim after flowering to keep it neat – or earlier if you want the fragrant flowerheads for drying.

Leucothoe fontanesiana 'Rainbow' Switch ivy
◑ ● ◓ pH ↓ ✿ ❖ YEAR-ROUND
H 1.5m (5ft) S 2m (6ft)

This colourful evergreen shrub is ideal for those difficult, deeply shaded spots where other plants tend to struggle. Its only requirements are acid soil and a reliable supply of moisture, which it repays handsomely by producing a dense thicket of arching, reddish stems swathed in leaves that are heavily marbled with cream and pink; it also has bunches of white flowers in spring.

Magnolia stellata 'Water Lily' Star magnolia
○ ◑ pH ↓ ✿ ❖ EARLY to MID-SPRING
H 3m (10ft) S 4m (13ft)

Truly a 'star', this magnolia is the perfect shrub for smaller gardens, where it is often grown standing on its own to show off its early flowers. And they're well worth it, being up to 12cm (5in) across and purest white, with lots of narrow petals that curve inwards like a water lily. They sit along bare branches, creating a wonderful picture to raise the spirits after winter, and are also fragrant.

Osmanthus × burkwoodii
○ ◑ ❖ MID- to LATE SPRING
H and S 3m (10ft)

Slow, dense growth and dark, glossy evergreen leaves make this an excellent hedging plant where space is tight, but its overriding attraction must be the masses of tiny, honey-scented white flowers that are borne in starry clusters in spring. Trim hedges after flowering, or allow an individual shrub to go its own way – it will take a very long time to outgrow its allotted space.

Osmanthus heterophyllus 'Goshiki'
○ ◑ ❖ YEAR-ROUND
H 3m (10ft) S 2m (6ft)

Goshiki means 'five colours': the spiny, holly-like leaves of this bell-shaped evergreen are marbled and mottled in various shades of green and yellow, while the young foliage is tinted bronze as well. The overall effect is bright and uplifting, especially in the winter months and if grown in full sun. The flowers, produced in autumn, are rather inconspicuous, but they make up for this by being sweetly fragrant.

Phormium 'Yellow Wave'
○ ❄ ❖ YEAR-ROUND
H 2.5m (8ft) S 2m (6ft)

This arching evergreen slowly makes a large clump of broad, yellow-and-green striped leaves and is a fantastic focal point, perhaps at the corner of a lawn or building. It isn't particularly fussy about positioning: you can grow it in the damp soil beside a pond, or in drier conditions in a coastal garden, where it looks especially at home. It benefits from a protective mulch in winter.

Photinia × fraseri 'Little Red Robin'

◯ ◑ ❄ ❖ SPRING

H and S 1m (40in)

This little shrub has a brilliant spring display provided by sharply vertical young shoots that bear rich wine-red leaves, which together create the illusion (from a distance!) that it is in flower. The foliage fades to a ruddy bronze and then turns green as it ages. Grow this compact evergreen among other shrubs for protection; choose a position that allows the photinia to fade into the background after its striking show.

Picea glauca var. *albertiana* 'Conica' White spruce

◯ pH ↓ ❖ YEAR-ROUND

H 1–2m (3–6ft) S 1.2m (4ft)

There is one very good reason to grow this conifer and that's its conical shape, which makes it a great focal point in the garden all year round. The plant grows slowly, plumping up gradually and adding rounded layers of texture to its outline as it goes. Plant this evergreen in a place where the soil never gets too dry; otherwise, the deep-green needles may brown and drop.

Pinus mugo 'Winter Gold'

Dwarf mountain pine

◯ ❖ WINTER

H 1m (40in) S 3m (10ft)

It is worth being particularly careful when choosing the site for this lovely dwarf form of the evergreen mountain pine. In winter, its needles are the colour of rolled gold and look their very best – all burnished and shining – when illuminated from behind by the low winter sun. For the rest of the year the foliage reverts to quiet green, creating an ideal background or accent among low-growing summer performers.

Physocarpus opulifolius 'Diabolo' Ninebark

◯ ◑ pH ↓ ❖ SPRING to AUTUMN

H and S 2m (6ft)

The richly coloured, deep-burgundy foliage of this fast-growing shrub has a lustrous sheen. In early summer, mounded domes of button-like white blooms open from red buds, giving a contrasting two-tone effect. Both foliage and flowers are wonderful for flower arrangements – and there are purple-bronze fruits in autumn, too. Place it among paler plants so its eye-catching qualities are thrown into sharp relief.

Pieris japonica 'Carnaval'

◯ ◑ pH ↓ 🌿 ❖ SPRING

H 1.5m (5ft) S 1m (40in)

Attractive all year, with its pink-flushed, white-edged evergreen leaves, this neat shrub really comes into its own in spring, with its dazzling, two-part display. First come generous panicles of small, ivory-white flowers (reminiscent of lily-of-the-valley), which are clustered together for maximum impact. These are followed by vivid red young leaves, which are even more attention-grabbing. Altogether, this plant is excellent value for gardens on acid soil.

Pittosporum tenuifolium 'Irene Paterson' Kohuhu

◯ ◑ ❄ ❖ YEAR-ROUND

H 1.2m (4ft) S 1.5m (5ft)

The creamy-white mottling and marbling on the leaves of this slow-growing evergreen is so plentiful that it can completely overwhelm any remnants of green. The overall effect is of a glossy mound of near-white. The colouring is best in full sun, and this little shrub needs a sheltered site, too: nestle it among plainer evergreens that will offer both protection and contrast.

Platycladus orientalis 'Aurea Nana'
◯ ❖ YEAR-ROUND
H 2m (6ft) S 1m (40in)

Formerly known as *Thuja orientalis* 'Aurea Nana', this little barrel-shaped conifer is incredibly slow-growing. It tends to sit around the 60cm (24in) mark seemingly forever, so is ideal for a tiny space, such as a courtyard garden or raised bed. The evergreen foliage is arranged to give a rippling, vertical striped effect that catches the eye, making it a good choice for a focal point. The yellow-green colour fades to bronze shades in winter.

Prunus incisa 'Kojo-no-mai'
Fuji cherry
◯ ❖ EARLY to MID-SPRING, AUTUMN
H and S 2.5m (8ft)

This truly is a gem among ornamental cherries, not least for being a compact shrub rather than a tree. Along the interestingly twisty twigs, fat buds open to a profusion of palest pink to white blossom that is produced reliably, year after year, even under tough conditions. There's also a crop of dark purple fruits in autumn, and good orange-red colour before the leaves fall.

Rosmarinus officinalis 'Miss Jessopp's Upright' Rosemary
◯ ❄ ❖ MID-SPRING to EARLY SUMMER
H 2m (6ft) S 1m (40in)

The common rosemary tends to have a rather untidy habit, which makes it difficult to accommodate in a small space. This upright version has the same pretty, purple-blue flowers and intensely aromatic, needle-like evergreen foliage but without the sprawl. It is particularly suitable for a sheltered spot beside the back door, where year-round clipping of sprigs for use in the kitchen will ensure the bush remains tidy.

Potentilla fruticosa 'Primrose Beauty'
◯ ❖ LATE SPRING to MID-AUTUMN
H 1m (40in) S 1.5m (5ft)

For sheer length of flowering, the shrubby potentillas are hard to beat. Given a sunny, well-drained spot, they are also very reliable and unfussy – their only drawback lies in the twiggy brown tangle the bushes become in winter. This variety has pale yellow flowers with a simple beauty that really does evoke wild primroses; there are others available in reds, oranges, pinks and white.

Rhododendron 'Patty Bee'
◯ ◗ pH ↓ ❀ ❖ EARLY to MID-SPRING
H and S 75cm (30in)

This little beauty of a plant would happily grace any garden on acid soil. In spring, its rounded dome of foliage is completely smothered by trusses of large, pale yellow flowers. The leaves, although evergreen, turn purple-bronze in winter. Unlike her larger, woodland cousins, 'Patty Bee' has alpine origins and enjoys sunbathing – as long as her roots remain moist.

Sarcococca confusa
Christmas box
◗ ● ❀ ❖ WINTER
H 2m (6ft) S 1m (40in)

This neat evergreen is useful on several counts: it tolerates a position in deep shade, it produces lots of fragrant little flowers in the depths of winter, and the glossy black berries that follow remain on the bush for a long time. Plant it in a sheltered spot alongside a path or doorway, so its wonderful scent can be appreciated rather than being wafted away on the wind.

Skimmia japonica 'Magic Marlot'

◐ ● ✿ ☀ YEAR-ROUND

H 50cm (20in) S 75cm (30in)

Variegated foliage ensures that this very useful, compact shrub catches the eye throughout the year, but it puts on a particularly wonderful show in the dark months, between autumn and spring. The display begins with the appearance of large, domed clusters of creamy buds that gradually turn rich red as winter progresses, finally opening to deliciously fragrant, white flowers in spring. It is small enough to be grown in a pot, too.

Spiraea japonica 'Firelight'

○ ✿ SPRING to SUMMER

H and S 1.5m (5ft)

Like all spiraeas, this is a completely trouble-free plant that will fit easily into any mixed or shrub border. The foliage goes through several stages: bright yellow in spring, becoming flushed with red, which persists as the leaves turn greener through the summer. Frothy purple-mauve flowerheads appear as a vibrant contrast in early summer. The ensemble looks good against darker, or purple-leaved, shrubs.

Syringa 'Red Pixie' Lilac

○ ✿ LATE SPRING

H and S 1.5m (5ft)

There was a time when lilacs were suitable only for large gardens, but newer versions such as 'Red Pixie' can happily be accommodated in more modest plots. In late spring, the bush is covered with cones of rich-red buds that open to pale pink flowers – but it's really all about the delicious fragrance, which, as with all lilacs, is truly overpowering.

Viburnum tinus 'Eve Price'

Laurustinus

○ ◐ ✿ LATE WINTER to SPRING

H and S 3m (10ft)

A sturdy, dense evergreen shrub, 'Eve Price' decorates the coldest days with robust heads of small white flowers, which open from carmine buds to create a pretty contrast. As other plants pick up and begin to perform, this one is happy to take a back seat, providing a neutral, dark green backdrop – with a few blue-black berries – for flowers and foliage of any colour.

Weigela florida 'Wine and Roses'

○ ◐ ✿ SPRING to SUMMER

H and S 2m (6ft)

Deep rose-pink flowers always look exciting against purple foliage, and here both are combined in one easy-to-please plant. The burgundy leaves deepen to near-black as summer days lengthen, unlike many other dark-leaved shrubs (including some weigelas) that fade to green. Place this power-packed shrub among paler, greener neighbours that will provide it with a gentle background.

Yucca filamentosa 'Bright Edge'

○ ◇ ✿ YEAR-ROUND

H 75cm (30in) S 1.5m (5ft)

This bold evergreen yucca has a rigid fan of spiky, blue-green leaves with broad yellow margins. It flowers every now and then too, producing a tall spike of nodding white flowers from mid- to late summer. Most yuccas love hot, dry conditions and, with their rather exotic, cactus-like appearance, this is where they look their best.

Easy-care roses

Roses are probably the most popular garden plants, and an excellent choice for weekend gardeners. Take no notice of their undeserved reputation for requiring pampering and succumbing to diseases. The roses listed here are every bit as healthy, disease-resistant and reliable as other garden plants and cannot be beaten for the quality and quantity of their flowers – these are all repeat-flowering.

Rosa 'Bonica'
○ ◗ ✿ SUMMER to AUTUMN
H 85cm (34in) S 1.2m (4ft)

Dainty sprays of small, lightly fragrant, soft-pink, semi-double flowers produced abundantly amid dark green foliage and followed by red hips, make this tough modern Shrub rose a good choice for the weekend gardener. The wider-than-high shape of the bush means that it is superb for providing ground cover. Alternatively, plant it in a mixed border for a reliable, summer-long display.

Rosa Flower Carpet series
○ ✿ SUMMER to AUTUMN
H 75cm (30in) S 1.2m (4ft)

The Flower Carpet series of roses are all vigorous, semi-evergreen, low-growing shrubs with glossy, dark green leaves and, through summer and into autumn, a good supply of large sprays of semi-double flowers. They tolerate poor, dry soil and are excellent for ground cover or adorning the side of a raised bed. Colours include pink (called Pink Flower Carpet, shown above), coral, white, yellow, scarlet and amber.

Rosa 'Absolutely Fabulous'
○ ◖ ✿ SUMMER to AUTUMN
H 75cm (30in) S 60cm (24in)

This little Floribunda rose is perfectly suited to a small garden. Its clusters of shapely and slightly ruffled, clear butter-yellow blooms are produced over a very long period and have a delightful liquorice-like scent. The bush is disease-resistant, with a regular and neat habit, so it is great in a pot on a sunny patio or any bright spot in the garden.

Rosa 'Darcey Bussell'
○ ◖ ✿ SUMMER to AUTUMN
H 90cm (3ft) S 60cm (24in)

Named after the talented ballerina, this English rose has perfectly formed, fully double, deep-crimson flowers that take on a mauve cast just before the petals fall. The flowers are produced in clusters and have a strong fragrance that is distinctly fruity. Short, bushy growth and very healthy, disease-resistant foliage make this an excellent rose for the front of a bed or border, or even for a good-sized container.

Rosa 'Fru Dagmar Hastrup'
○ ◖ ✿ SUMMER to AUTUMN
H 1m (40in) S 1.2m (4ft)

Rugosa roses make a dense thicket of prickly stems bearing tough, wrinkled leaves and large flowers that are often followed by red, tomato-shaped hips. All this makes them desirable roses for hedging. 'Fru Dagmar Hastrup' is a lovely variety, producing clove-scented, simple cup-shaped, pale pink flowers all summer and dark red hips in autumn.

Rosa 'Iceberg'
○ 🌿 ❖ SUMMER to AUTUMN
H 80cm (32in) S 65cm (26in)

One of the best and most popular modern roses (there is also a climbing form), 'Iceberg' has masses of large flower clusters, each bloom well-rounded and double with a pleasant, though light, fresh fragrance. The bush also has glossy, pale green leaves and is vigorous yet compact, making it ideal for an informal hedge. It also looks completely at home in a mixed border.

Rosa 'Queen of Sweden'
○ 🌿 ❖ SUMMER to AUTUMN
H 1m (40in) S 75cm (30in)

A real little beauty, this upright, bushy English rose is perfect where space is limited, as in a narrow border or raised bed. It can also be used as hedging and is happy being grown in a container. It has disease-resistant, dark green foliage and cup-shaped, apricot-pink blooms that fade to delicate pale pink. The fragrance is slight, but to compensate the flowers are weather-resistant and freely produced.

Rosa 'Rhapsody in Blue'
○ 🌿 ❖ SUMMER to EARLY AUTUMN
H 1.5m (5ft) S 1m (40in)

The elusive 'blue' rose is still just that, but this upright shrub comes quite close. The semi-double blooms open to a good shade of purple-blue (albeit with a hint of red about it) and fade to mauve-grey – both contrast nicely with the golden stamens inside. The flower clusters are plentiful, and there is a strong fragrance as well.

Rosa 'Sweet Dream'
○ 🌿 ❖ SUMMER to AUTUMN
H and S 50cm (20in)

With its upright but bushy growth, this very popular Patio rose is ideal for growing in a pot, or you could try it as a low hedge in the garden. The leaves are shiny and dark green, and the pretty, lightly fragrant flowers are like shallow, open cups full of apricot-pink petals neatly arranged in layers. They are borne in large clusters throughout summer.

Rosa 'The Pilgrim'
○ ◑ 🌿 ❖ SUMMER to AUTUMN
H 1.2m (4ft) S 1m (40in)

An upright English rose that eventually forms a pretty vase shape, 'The Pilgrim' has strong, healthy growth and dark green leaves. Its flowers are pure but light yellow, with many small petals opening to form a flat, evenly shaped bloom. Its fragrance is delightful, mixing English rose myrrh with the classic Tea scent, and can be enjoyed through summer and into autumn. There is also a fast-growing climbing form.

Rosa 'Warm Welcome'
○ 🌿 ❖ SUMMER to AUTUMN
H 2.5m (8ft) S 1.5m (5ft)

This is a miniature Patio climbing rose that is semi-evergreen with dark green, pointed leaves that are bronze-tinted when young. The lightly fragrant, semi-double flowers are borne in clusters and are a surprising rich scarlet with gold at the base of each petal. It is a perfect climber where space is at a premium – you could grow it over an obelisk or drape it over a low wall.

Easy-care climbers and wall shrubs

Most climbers and wall shrubs are easy to care for, provided you choose the right plant for the situation, but the ones suggested here are particularly undemanding. They add height, colour and form to the garden, and also create screens and disguise unsightly walls and fences. Climbers are ideal for growing through other plants to fill the gaps between seasons of interest.

Akebia quinata Chocolate vine
○ ◑ ❖ SPRING
H 10m (33ft) S 2m (6ft)

A rather floppy twining climber, the chocolate vine is suitable for growing into a tree, over a rustic garden structure or against a warm wall: give it some help, especially to begin with. It has lush, rounded leaflets that are semi-evergreen – they often develop interesting purple tints in winter – and clusters of pendent flowers in an unusual shade of pinkish purple-brown, with a spicy vanilla scent.

Chaenomeles speciosa 'Geisha Girl' Quince
○ ◑ ❖ SPRING
H and S 2.5m (8ft)

Ornamental quinces are invaluable wall shrubs for the generous early-spring colour they bring to the garden. 'Geisha Girl' continues flowering for a good couple of months, its bare branches smothered with double, soft apricot-pink blooms until the glossy leaves appear. The plants flower on old wood, so do a bit of careful pruning to remove some of the newer growth and ensure the flowers are in full view.

Clematis cirrhosa var. purpurascens 'Freckles'
○ ◑ ❄ ❧ ❖ WINTER to EARLY SPRING
H 3m (10ft) S 2m (6ft)

The earliest of all winter-flowering clematis, 'Freckles' is often in bloom by Christmas. Each nodding, creamy bell is heavily speckled brownish red inside and is best viewed from below, so grow it over an arch or pergola. The site should be sheltered, so you can capture the light fragrance, but also to protect the plant. This plant flowers on old wood, so just cut out anything dead or damaged.

Clematis 'Markham's Pink'
○ ◑ ❧ ❖ SPRING to EARLY SUMMER
H 2m (6ft) S 1.5m (5ft)

The powder-pink blooms of this little climber are lovely for creating a subtle contrast with pale yellow daffodils. Fluffy seedheads appear after hot summers. 'Markham's Pink' is related to Clematis macropetala, which has similar flowers in violet-blue. Other relatives include: 'White Swan' (pure white; compact) and 'Jan Lindmark' (mauve-pink). The macropetalas rarely suffer from clematis wilt (sudden dieback in the stems) and need no more than an annual tidy-up.

Clematis 'Polish Spirit'
○ ◑ ❧ ❖ MIDSUMMER to AUTUMN
H 3m (10ft) S 1.5m (5ft)

This late-flowering clematis bears masses of smallish, deep-purple flowers with red anthers, perfect for adding late colour to an obelisk, fence or arch. Like all Clematis viticella relatives, it is resistant to clematis wilt (and planting deeply helps to ward it off). Other C. viticella relatives include: 'Alba Luxurians' (green-tipped white, black anthers) and 'Mme Julia Correvon' (wine-red, yellow anthers). Cut back old stems to a strong pair of buds in spring.

Cotoneaster horizontalis
○ ❖ LATE SPRING to EARLY SUMMER, AUTUMN
H 2m (6ft) S 1.5m (5ft)

This little wall shrub is a traditional favourite that can be seen thriving in many old gardens. Its most striking feature is the herringbone pattern of its branches, making it ideal for growing against a low wall or over a bank. The little white flowers are very attractive to bees and are followed by masses of red berries, which draw in the birds. There is also good autumn leaf colour, in orange and red shades.

Euonymus fortunei 'Emerald Gaiety'
○ ◑ ❖ YEAR-ROUND
H 1m (40in) S 1.5m (5ft)

Ideal for adding some pizzazz to a dull corner, this low-growing, variegated evergreen shrub lends itself readily to training up against a wall, where it will provide dense cover. It can also trail among other plants or droop from a low wall. The matt green leaves have irregular white margins that develop contrasting pink tints in winter. In full sun the foliage will be brighter, but the soil needs to be moister.

Hedera colchica 'Dentata Variegata' Persian ivy
○ ◑ 🍂 ❖ YEAR-ROUND
H and S 5m (16ft)

Big, hearty evergreen leaves splashed with creamy white are the valuable feature of this vigorous ivy, which looks especially good against a red-brick wall. (Ivies will not damage sound brickwork, although they may take advantage of already loose mortar and old paintwork.) Use it to brighten a corner in partial or dappled shade: in deeper shade, the variegation will suffer.

Hedera helix 'Glacier'
○ ◑ 🍂 ❖ YEAR-ROUND
H and S 2m (6ft)

This is a neat little climber that can be grown vertically against a wall or horizontally as ground cover. It also looks good over a bank and is not so dense that other plants cannot peek through it. The evergreen leaves are almost triangular and grey-green, variegated with silver-grey and cream. The overall impression is very pretty – place it where the intricate patterning can be enjoyed close up.

Lonicera periclymenum 'Serotina'
Late Dutch honeysuckle
○ ◑ 🍂 ❖ MIDSUMMER to EARLY AUTUMN
H and S 7m (23ft)

Honeysuckles are versatile twining climbers that can be grown against a wall, over a fence, or through a large shrub or small tree. Choose a situation that allows the sweet fragrance of the flowers to be enjoyed at nose height. 'Serotina' has a strong scent, especially in the evening, and produces its red-purple and cream flowers over a particularly long period.

Trachelospermum jasminoides
Star jasmine
○ ◑ ❄ ❖ MID- to LATE SUMMER
H and S 6m (20ft)

This slow-growing twiner has dark evergreen leaves that adopt attractive bronze shades in winter. In summer it produces plentiful simple yet beautiful, pure white flowers whose unbelievably powerful fragrance will stop passers-by in their tracks. Although it is surprisingly tough, it does best in a sheltered spot against a warm wall. Put a seat nearby and wallow in the scent.

Easy-care perennials

Perennial plants are usually herbaceous, which means they die down over winter and regrow in spring, although some are evergreen and provide interest in winter. Unlike some perennials, the ones included here are well behaved and require no more from you than a bit of light dead-heading – an easy job (*see* page 43) – and, very occasionally, the provision of some support (*see* page 40).

Achillea filipendulina 'Gold Plate'
○ ❖ EARLY SUMMER to EARLY AUTUMN
H 1.2m (4ft) S 45cm (18in)

With its huge, plate-like, bright golden-yellow flowerheads, this yarrow demands attention and should get it. The shape of the flowerheads makes them ideal for contrasting with many other flower shapes in a mixed bed. It looks especially good teamed with spikes of flowers in rich, deep blues, such as aconitums. 'Cloth of Gold' is similar but taller, at 1.5m (5ft).

Aconitum 'Spark's Variety'
Monkshood
○ ◑ ♦ ❖ MID- to LATE SUMMER
H 1.5m (5ft) S 45cm (18in)

This monkshood is a superb back-of-the-border plant, its spires of hooded, deep violet-blue flowers rising to great heights above lowlier subjects. The rich, dark colour complements beautifully the strong yellows of achilleas or the yellow-orange of heleniums, and also looks good among tall ornamental grasses. A warning: all parts of this plant are toxic if ingested, and contact with the foliage may irritate skin.

Alchemilla mollis Lady's mantle
○ ◑ ❖ EARLY SUMMER to EARLY AUTUMN
H 60cm (24in) S 75cm (30in)

This archetypal cottage-garden plant looks especially appealing after rain or a heavy dew, when droplets captured by the softly hairy, folded leaves sparkle gently in the sun. It also produces frothy, lime-green flowerheads that go on and on and are perfect for cutting. Lady's mantle will seed itself prettily around the garden. It is a great edging plant and looks wonderful with almost all other perennials.

Alstroemeria Little Miss series
Dwarf Peruvian lily
○ ◑ ❄ ❖ EARLY SUMMER to EARLY AUTUMN
H 15–35cm (6–14in) S 45cm (18in)

A diminutive version of the well-known cut flower, this little perennial has been bred especially for smaller gardens, as well as for a long and reliable flowering period. It has miniature, lily-like flowers in a range of colours, most with yellow markings and dark flecks. Protect it with a winter mulch. Colours include: 'Little Miss Sophie' (white-and-pink bicolour), 'Little Miss Isabel' (deep red) and 'Little Miss Gina' (bright cherry-pink).

Aster dumosus 'Sapphire'
○ ◑ ♦ ❖ LATE SUMMER to MID-AUTUMN
H and S 50cm (20in)

Asters are valued for their abundant and bright, late-season flowers, and this one is a particularly beautiful lilac-blue. It also has disease-resistant foliage, a bushy, compact habit and a massed display of large, fluffy daisy flowers with yellow centres. It looks good with other late flowers, such as heleniums, and with purple-leaved heucheras or grasses. There are also white and pink varieties.

Astrantia 'Snow Star'
Hattie's pincushion
○ ◑ ◔ ✿ ❖ SUMMER
H 90cm (3ft) S 45cm (18in)

Astrantias have pretty flowers that consist of a central boss that looks a bit like a pincushion and is surrounded by a ruff of papery bracts. 'Snow Star' has a white 'pincushion' and green-tipped bracts – a subtle colouring that allows it to be slipped in among geraniums, heucheras and any number of other perennials. Astrantias are very good for cutting to bring indoors.

Bergenia 'Overture'
Elephant's ears
○ ◑ ✿ ❖ SPRING
H 35cm (14in) S 20cm (8in)

Larger bergenias can sprawl and spread, but this is a mini version that forms a really neat clump of smooth, rounded, evergreen leaves. The foliage takes on a lovely, heart-warming burgundy glow in winter. Columns of bright rose-pink flowers herald the spring, so select some companions from the lively palette of early bulbs, such as snowdrops and small daffodils, and other spring flowers.

Brunnera macrophylla 'Looking Glass'
◑ ✿ ❖ SPRING to AUTUMN
H and S 45cm (18in)

Dramatic, heart-shaped, all-silver leaves (with a tiny green rim) are this woodland plant's *raison d'être* and will enhance any lightly shaded area. It looks thoroughly comfortable nestling beneath a tree or airy shrub, especially with dark-leaved ground-cover plants, such as ajugas. In spring, rich-blue forget-me-not-like flowers dance above the foliage. Where shrubs or trees don't do the job for you, mulch with leaf mould every few years.

Dahlia 'Bishop of Llandaff'
○ ✿ ✿ ❖ MIDSUMMER to AUTUMN
H 1.2m (4ft) S 45cm (18in)

Dahlias do need some work in that you have to protect young growth from slugs and the tubers from frost, but they will repay this effort with a sumptuous display of showy, colourful blooms over a long period. 'Bishop of Llandaff' is a particularly stunning variety, with dark red-black leaves and rich-red, semi-double flowers with gold anthers. Grow it with asters, heleniums or cannas.

Digitalis × mertonensis Foxglove
◑ ✿ ❖ LATE SPRING to EARLY SUMMER
H 90cm (3ft) S 30cm (12in)

This neat foxglove has the recognizable spires of thimble-shaped flowers, but in a unique, soft pinkish-buff shade. It comes true from seed (as long as there are no other foxgloves growing nearby), so your stocks will increase rapidly if you allow it to self-sow. It looks perfect in a woodland setting, where it makes a good companion for ferns and the foliage of already-flowered hellebores.

Epimedium × versicolor
Barrenwort
○ ◑ ✿ ❖ MID- to LATE SPRING
H 20–30cm (8–12in) S 30cm (12in)

This evergreen ground-covering gem impresses twice over in spring: with the copper-red and brown tints of its heart-shaped young leaves, and its dainty, muted pink-and-yellow spurred flowers held high on long, thin stems. It looks good with tiny spring bulbs like scillas and muscari. Good varieties with similar leaf colouring include: 'Cupreum' (copper-red flowers), 'Neosulphureum' (pale yellow) and 'Sulphureum' (darker yellow with longer spurs).

Euphorbia characias subsp. *wulfenii* Spurge

○ ❄ ◊ ❖ EARLY SPRING to SUMMER

H and S 1.2m (4ft)

This spurge is an architectural evergreen *par excellence*, so long as you can give it a warm, dry spot. The tall stems of blue-green, whorled, almost succulent foliage are startling enough; add huge domed heads of acid-green flowers and you have a real conversation-stopper. Set it as a focal point against a wall or place a pair either side of a simple bench or gate.

Gaura lindheimeri 'Rosyjane'

○ ❖ LATE SPRING to EARLY AUTUMN

H 75cm (30in) S 60cm (24in)

Graceful, airy plants for a sunny border, gauras have the added advantage of being drought-tolerant. Their flowers, hovering on wiry stems above willowy foliage ('Rosyjane's are white with cerise-pink edging), go on and on, and are a real draw for bees. Give the plant space to lean its floaty stems gently over pathways and its bedfellows, which could include geraniums and nepetas.

Geranium 'Rozanne' Cranesbill

○ ◑ ❖ SUMMER

H 60cm (24in) S 1m (40in)

Most geraniums are good garden plants, but 'Rozanne' is a particularly fine performer. It makes a mound of finely cut, velvety foliage that turns bronze-red in autumn, but the crowning glory is its large flowers. These are a brilliant blue, with violet veining and a white centre, and are produced repeatedly during the summer – a shearing in midsummer will freshen the foliage and encourage the production of lots more blooms.

Helenium 'Moerheim Beauty' Sneezeweed

○ ❖ SUMMER

H 90cm (36in) S 60cm (24in)

This classic tall border plant is a brilliant performer, with its daisy flowers in shades of copper-red, tawny brown and yellow. In good seasons it may start to bloom in early or midsummer and will continue right through to the end of summer. For similar flowers, lasting later into the year, pick 'Wyndley' (yellow with copper markings) or 'Rubinzwerg' (rich dark red). All are good for cutting.

Helleborus foetidus Stinking hellebore

◑ 🍃 ❖ MIDWINTER to MID-SPRING

H 60cm (24in) S 45cm (18in)

Luckily, to release the foetid odour from this plant you would need to crush the leaves and sniff them. Instead, it's better to admire the handsome toothed foliage *in situ*, together with the clusters of fascinating pale green, nodding flowers: turn them gently upwards for closer inspection. This long-lived perennial thrives in a woodland setting or mixed shrub border. Brunneras and epimediums make good companions.

Helleborus × hybridus Lenten rose

◑ 🍃 ❖ MIDWINTER to MID-SPRING

H and S 45cm (18in)

The lovely Lenten rose comes in a range of colours, from white through green, and pink and red to almost black. Shown above is an Ashwood Garden hybrid, and there are many other named varieties, including 'Black Beauty' and 'Peggy Ballard' (deep plum-purple). You can also purchase 'pot luck' mixed seedlings, which will provide you with a stunning, inexpensive display. For maximum flower power, remove the old leaves as the flower buds appear.

Heuchera Coral flower
○ ◐ ❄ (some) ❖ YEAR-ROUND
H 30cm (12in) S 45cm (18in) (taller when in flower)

With their often vibrant base colours, variegation and marbling, heucheras make striking evergreen or semi-evergreen ground cover for the front of a border. They also produce dainty wands of bell-shaped flowers in every shade from white, green and pink to scarlet and vermilion. Among the many attention-grabbing varieties are 'Peach Flambé' (peach-pink leaves, purple in winter, and white flowers; shown above) and 'Plum Pudding' (metallic silver-purple foliage and silvery flowers).

Nepeta × faassenii Catmint
○ ◐ ❖ EARLY SUMMER to EARLY AUTUMN
H and S 45cm (18in)

This pretty catmint is soft and appealing in every aspect – cats certainly think so, and love rolling in its mounds of aromatic, hairy silver-grey leaves. Clouds of pretty, pale lavender-blue flowers are produced throughout summer, especially if it is given a haircut when the first flush of blooms begins to look tired. Position it where the hazy stems can tumble gently over a patio, path or gravel.

Ophiopogon planiscapus 'Nigrescens' Lilyturf
○ ◐ pH↓ 🌿 ❖ YEAR-ROUND
H 20cm (8in) S 30cm (12in)

Strictly speaking, this isn't a grass, but it certainly gives that impression. It is very striking, with gently spreading clumps of near-black, arching leaves that look superb growing in paler gravel, especially alongside contrasting silver-leaved sun-lovers. It also looks good with ferns in dappled shade. For added interest there are little purplish-white, bell-shaped flowers in summer, followed by dark blue-black fruits.

Penstemon 'Andenken an Friedrich Hahn'
○ ◐ ❖ MIDSUMMER to MID-AUTUMN
H 75cm (30in) S 60cm (24in)

One of the hardiest of all penstemons, this perennial may be cut back by the severest cold but will almost always return to robust growth in spring. It is tallish but generally self-supporting, so shouldn't collapse over more modest neighbours. The lovely, rich wine-red flowers look excellent with grasses or silvery leaved plants, such as lavender or catmint. You will also find it listed by its old name 'Garnet'.

Penstemon 'Stapleford Gem'
○ ◐ ❖ MIDSUMMER to MID-AUTUMN
H 60cm (24in) S 45cm (18in)

In cold areas you will need to give this penstemon a protective winter mulch, but it's definitely worth the effort. The foxglove-like flowers are an interesting blend of several soft colours – pale lilac-blue, white and purple-pink – and are produced over a long period. They will harmonize with almost any other flower colour you like, and will also provide gentle relief from more strident late-season blooms.

Phlox paniculata Perennial phlox
○ ◐ ◆ ❖ SUMMER to AUTUMN
H and S 1.2m (4ft)

Phlox are large-scale, showy border plants for reliably moist soils. They have big heads of little flowers in shades of white, pink, red or purple, often with a contrasting darker eye and sometimes sweetly scented. Taller varieties will need staking; shorter ones include 'Bright Eyes' (soft pink with a crimson eye) and 'Norah Leigh' (pale lilac with cream-variegated leaves; shown above). Both are fragrant and mildew-resistant.

Pulmonaria longifolia 'Bertram Anderson' Lungwort
◐ ◐ ◑ ✿ ❖ LATE WINTER to LATE SPRING
H and S 30cm (12in)

Lungworts are often among the first perennials to bloom, while their attractive foliage makes good ground cover among trees or shrubs, in a wild garden, or at the front of a shady border. There are many excellent cultivars, but this one has exceptionally long, narrow leaves boldly spotted with silvery white and really intense, bright blue flowers, so is a doubly good choice.

Pulsatilla vulgaris Pasque flower
○ ❖ SPRING
H and S 15–20cm (6–8in)

For a shimmering, silvery effect on a rock garden, bank or scree, this lovely native plant is a real winner. Feathery light green leaves, silky-hairy purple flowers and silvery, plume-like seed-heads all play their part. Pasque flowers can sometimes be difficult to establish, so plant them when small and leave undisturbed. Good varieties include f. *alba* (white), 'Barton's Pink' (silver-pink) and 'Röde Klokke' (deep red).

Saxifraga × *urbium* London pride
◐ ● ✿ ❖ SUMMER
H 15cm (6in) S 60cm (24in)

Even in poor soils, this unassuming cottage-garden favourite spreads its neat rosettes of spoon-shaped leaves to make a solid mat. Never invasive, it is useful for ground cover, especially in a dry, shady area such as near shrubs and trees. Little, pretty pinkish-white flowers float on wiry stems above the leaves in summer. 'Variegata' has strong yellow splashes on the foliage to enliven even the dreariest corner.

Sedum 'Herbstfreude' Ice plant
○ ❖ EARLY AUTUMN
H and S 50cm (20in)

There are two striking features to this handsome perennial: fleshy, succulent, grey-green leaves and large, slightly domed, rich-pink flowerheads, produced at a time when many plants are slipping quietly into dormancy. The flowers are loved by butterflies, which gather on them in surprising numbers. Eventually the flowerheads fade to brown, providing interesting structure into winter. Like many other sedums, it is drought-tolerant.

Stachys byzantina Lamb's ears
○ ❖ SPRING to AUTUMN
H 45cm (18in) S 60cm (24in)

A cottage classic, lamb's ears is named for its densely white-woolly, grey-green leaves. Ideal in leaf for informal ground cover in a gravel garden or as edging, it also produces white stems of small, woolly magenta flowers in summer. These are a favourite with bees. Grow it under roses or with one of the airy gauras. 'Big Ears' has larger leaves. 'Silver Carpet' is non-flowering, with intensely silvery foliage.

Verbascum 'Jackie in Pink' Mullein
○ ❖ SUMMER
H 60cm (24in) S 40cm (16in)

Mulleins are often extremely tall and very lovely, but not always practical for small gardens. However, this dwarf version will fit into any space. It has a neat rosette of leaves and vertical stems of warm salmon-pink flowers, each with a dark eye. Its size means it is perfect for a spot at the front of a border. Its 'sister plant', 'Jackie in Yellow', is just a shade stronger than primrose.

Easy-care ferns and grasses

Ferns (this page) and grasses (opposite) are excellent for providing focal points and foliage textures. Ferns do well under trees. Many grasses die to soft beige in autumn, and both foliage and flowerheads can be left to decorate the winter garden. Remove old growth of both ferns and grasses in spring, as the new growth starts. It's a small price to pay for these lovely plants.

Asplenium scolopendrium
Hart's tongue fern
◑ pH↑ 🍂 ❖ YEAR-ROUND
H and S 60cm (24in)

A native of rocky streamsides, this evergreen fern has glossy, bright green, tongue-like fronds that grow outwards and upwards. Its unusually solid form makes a good contrast to moisture-loving wildflowers or other ferns with more filigree fronds beneath trees or beside a pond. It also makes a low-level architectural focal point among shrubs and perennials in a shady mixed border.

Dryopteris erythrosora
Buckler fern
◑ 💧 🍂 ❖ SPRING to AUTUMN
H 60cm (24in) S 38cm (15in)

Given a sheltered and reliably moist site, this little fern makes a lovely subtle contribution to a semi-shaded area. It is particularly striking early in the year, when its new fronds unfurl a surprising copper-pink. Later they become simple mid-green, but their horizontal arrangement continues to provide contrasting form among other more standard plant shapes and foliage styles in the border.

Dryopteris filix-mas Male fern
◑ ● 💧 🍂 ❖ SPRING to AUTUMN
H and S 1m (40in)

Don't overlook this graceful fern's garden potential just because it is so common in the wild. Although it enjoys damp soil, it is a true stoic and will also grow in dry conditions – even surviving when tucked in close to the trunk of a tree or at the base of a hedge, where conditions are always truly tough. Grow several plants in a group along with spring bulbs and hellebores.

Matteuccia struthiopteris
Shuttlecock fern
◑ 💧 pH↓ 🍂 ❖ SPRING to AUTUMN
H 1.2m (4ft) S 1m (40in)

This beautiful big fern reproduces by spreading its rhizomes horizontally, so that new 'shuttlecocks' of fronds appear about 20cm (8in) from the parent plant. Its other name is ostrich fern, which is equally descriptive, as the upright leaves arch elegantly and have a feathery form. It will increase slowly in dry spots under trees, and more quickly in a damp border or beside a pond.

Polystichum setiferum
'Plumosomultilobum'
Soft shield fern
◑ ● 🍂 ❖ YEAR-ROUND
H 1.2m (4ft) 90cm (3ft)

Ignore the complicated name and choose this plant for its thick, soft-looking, moss-like fronds. Its shape is unusual, its wide-spreading leaves varying in length and often slightly curved, giving the impression of elegant disorder. Plant it in shady spots with other ferns, hellebores and epimediums, all of which will complement its attractive form.

Carex elata 'Aurea'
Bowles's golden sedge
○ ◑ ◐ 🌢 ❖ SPRING to AUTUMN
H 70cm (28in) S 45cm (18in)

With golden leaves that have narrow green margins, this grass arches gently upwards, occasionally bending out and down, giving an informal effect. In late spring it bears slim, silky brown flower spikes. The foliage colour – magnificent beside blue flowers, like those of hardy geraniums, and dark foliage – is sharpest in a sunny situation, but the soil must be moist. Choose this sedge for pondsides or areas prone to occasional flooding.

Festuca glauca Blue fescue
○ ❖ YEAR-ROUND
H 30cm (12in) S 25cm (10in)

The silvery shade of this small, dense evergreen grass becomes bluer as the sun gets stronger, so the colour deepens satisfyingly as summer moves on. It needs sharp drainage, so is completely at home in gravel or a raised bed. Named cultivars offer variations in tone and include 'Blaufuchs' (bright blue), 'Harz' (blue-green tipped purple) and 'Golden Toupee' (bright gold-green).

Hakonechloa macra 'Aureola'
○ ◑ ◐ 🍃 ❖ SPRING to AUTUMN
H 35cm (14in) S 40cm (16in)

This grass can take time to establish, but is worth the wait. Reminiscent of a mop of unruly hair, the clump produces bright yellow, green-striped leaves that look fresh all summer, then develop a red autumn flush before disappearing for the winter. The plant's compact habit makes it suitable for a restricted site – it will grow well in a container. Foliage colour is best in light shade.

Miscanthus sinensis 'Morning Light'
○ ❖ SPRING to AUTUMN
H 1.5m (5ft) S 1.2m (4ft)

A mammoth grass that enjoys plenty of sun and protection from excessive winter wet, this miscanthus makes a superb, eye-catching focal point. The blue-green foliage is especially narrow and has shimmering, silvered edges that enhance its slender appearance. Silky-hairy, reddish-brown flower plumes on tall stems wave gently in the autumn breeze and add to the plant's stature as its seasonal cycle draws to a close.

Pennisetum alopecuroides 'Hameln' Fountain grass
○ ❄ ❖ SUMMER to AUTUMN
H and S 30–90cm (1–3ft)

Like a fountain, the long, arching leaves of this beautiful evergreen grass cascade out from the centre. From summer to autumn the watery illusion is perfected by fuzzy, pink-brown flower spikes, which spray outwards from the tips of long, waving stems and are great for cutting and drying. Grow among hardier subjects in a mixed border and protect in winter with a mulch.

Stipa tenuissima Feathergrass
○ ❖ SPRING to AUTUMN
H 60cm (24in) S 30cm (12in)

The foliage of this delicate grass is filament-fine, allowing the whole plant to billow prettily in the slightest breeze. Throughout summer there is the added attraction of nodding, feathery flower plumes that start off greenish white and eventually turn buff-brown. These can be dried – or even dyed – to add depth to winter arrangements. Alternatively, leave them in place as a subtle overwintering attraction.

Easy-care bulbs

Most bulbs will perform without any input from the gardener. The easiest way to grow many of them is to let them become 'naturalized', leaving them to spread in informal drifts, particularly under trees or in grassy areas. Feed after flowering and allow them to die down naturally. Taller kinds, such as lilies, may need staking, while cannas require a winter mulch (*see* page 40), but they're worth the extra effort.

Anemone blanda blue shades
Wood anemone
◐ 🦋 ❖ SPRING
H and **S** 15cm (6in)

The little tubers quickly bulk up to form large clumps so, if you give this plant plenty of space to spread in the dappled shade beneath trees and shrubs, within a few years you will have sheets of beautiful rich-blue, gold-centred daisy flowers to greet the spring. Other recommended *Anemone blanda* varieties include: 'Charmer' (deep pink); 'White Splendour' (pure white); var. *rosea* 'Radar' (magenta with a white centre).

Chionodoxa luciliae
Glory of the snow
○ ❖ EARLY SPRING
H 15cm (6in) **S** 4cm (1¾in)

This is a charming little early bulb with star-shaped, white-centred blue flowers that will adapt to a variety of garden situations. Try it in a raised bed or in a trough, or allow it to self-seed into pretty carpets with other spring bulbs beneath deciduous trees and shrubs. *Chionodoxa* 'Pink Giant' is slighter taller and has delicate-looking, pink petals that fade almost to white at the centre.

Allium cristophii Star of Persia
○ ❖ EARLY SUMMER to AUTUMN
H 60cm (24in) **S** 20cm (8in)

Most ornamental onions make good garden plants, with their rounded heads of flowers, usually in shades of purple-pink, in a variety of sizes. This one has particularly striking, spiky and starry, metallic purple-pink flowers in heads that can be up to 20cm (8in) across. Use them in groups for greatest impact. After the flowers fade, the developing seedheads look good in a border, or they can be cut earlier and dried for use indoors.

Canna 'Phasion'
○ ❀ ❖ SUMMER to LATE AUTUMN
H 1.2–2m (4–6ft)

Cannas are rhizomatous plants that always look exotic, with their towering height, bold flowers in searing shades and magnificent, often coloured leaves. 'Phasion', also called 'Durban' or 'Tropicanna', is a brilliant example, with dramatic, dark green, red-and-orange striped leaves and scarlet-orange blooms. Grow several in a warm spot, perhaps on a patio, and take care to purchase virus-free stock. Lift for winter or grow in large, movable containers.

Cyclamen hederifolium
◐ 🦋 ❖ AUTUMN to SPRING
H 10cm (4in) **S** 15cm (6in)

Borne on slender stems, the nodding pink flowers of this small corm appear before the leaves to make a wonderful display in autumn beneath trees and shrubs. Over the years they will self-seed freely and spread. After the flowers have finished, heart-shaped leaves with silvery patterning appear and provide very pretty ground cover into spring. Grow under deciduous trees and shrubs or in a raised bed or container. Shown above is *C.* var. *hederifolium* f. *h.* 'Ruby Glow'.

Galanthus nivalis
Common snowdrop
◑ 🍂 ❖ MID- to LATE WINTER
H and S 10cm (4in)

Once the snowdrops begin to open, we can believe that winter is at last on the wane. Simple yet beautiful, pure white blooms with tiny green markings nod gently among arching foliage and spread steadily over the years beneath trees and shrubs, in grass, or through a border or rock garden. The double-flowered version f. *pleniflorus* 'Flore Pleno' is chubbier but just as lovely, and it spreads well too.

Lilium regale Royal lily
○ ❖ MIDSUMMER
H 1.5m (5ft) S 50cm (20in)

This is an easy-to-grow lily that can be slotted into any sunny border to provide height, style and, of course, wonderful fragrance. The big trumpet flowers are purest white with subtle burgundy-red stripes and bright golden anthers – definitely a regal combination. Best in large groups, they are obligingly easy to grow from freely produced seed, and the bulbs flower even when quite young.

Narcissus 'February Gold'
Daffodil
○ ◐ pH ↓ ❖ EARLY SPRING
H 30cm (12in) S 10cm (4in)

The name gives it away: this is a very early-flowering daffodil, a true herald of spring. It is vigorous and, although suitable for borders, is probably at its best naturalized in grass, where it spreads to produce swathes of bright golden-yellow blooms. For strong bulbs and good flowering the following year, do not cut or remove leaves until six weeks after the flowers have faded.

Narcissus 'Hawera' Daffodil
○ ◐ pH ↓ ❖ MID- to LATE SPRING
H 18cm (7in) S 10cm (4in)

Dainty, miniature narcissi like this one are ideal for planting in containers, troughs and window boxes as well as at the front of raised beds or borders. Several nodding, canary-yellow flowers with swept-back outer petals and a light fragrance are borne on each stem, so you don't need huge numbers of bulbs to create a massed effect.

Tulipa 'Lilac Perfection'
○ ❖ LATE SPRING
H 50cm (20in) S 20cm (8in)

Ruffled layers of warm lilac-pink petals form full, bowl-shaped blooms that sit well atop the blue-grey foliage of this tulip. The occasional white suffusion to a petal-tip adds to the informal effect. This is a tulip for a blowsy cottage-garden border rather than a stylized bedding scheme – cram it in among fresh new foliage and complementary spring flowers, such as forget-me-nots.

Tulipa 'Queen of Night'
○ ❖ LATE SPRING
H 60cm (24in) S 30cm (12in)

A tall tulip with velvety, dark maroon flowers, 'Queen of Night' adds an appropriate air of mystery to any planting scheme. The flower colour is unusual at this time of year and makes a powerful contrast with pale yellows, pinks and whites – provided by other tulips, for example – or against a bright background of golden or lime-green young foliage, such as euphorbia.

Easy-care annuals and other bedding

Bedding plants are perfect for filling gaps in beds and borders, as well as providing colour in containers for long periods over the summer and into autumn. Their needs are usually just plenty of water and regular dead-heading – and for that you get an abundance of lovely flowers wherever and whenever you need them.

Bacopa
○ ◑ ❀ pH ↓ ❖ EARLY SUMMER to EARLY AUTUMN
H 20cm (8in) S 60cm (24in)

Also known as *Sutera*, these are great trailing plants for baskets, window boxes and troughs. With their profusion of dainty, pale-toned fluted flowers, they are ideal for balancing a mix of strident colours and larger flowers. They also look wonderful planted on their own for a quieter, gentler scheme. Popular varieties include 'Snowflake' (shown above) and 'Snowtopia', both pure white; 'Bluetopia' is soft lilac.

Begonia Million Kisses series
○ ◑ ❀ pH ↓ 🍂 ❖ LATE SPRING to EARLY AUTUMN
H 40cm (16in) S 50cm (20in)

It is easy to be seduced by these begonias, which have individual names like 'Devotion' (hot red), 'Amour' (red with dark leaves), 'Elegance' (white with pink flushing) and 'Romance' (salmon; shown above). A profusion of elegant bell-shaped flowers on plants with luxuriant cascading growth makes them ideal for baskets and other containers, which they quickly fill. No trimming or dead-heading is required, and they are also heat- and drought-tolerant.

Calibrachoa Cabaret series
○ ❀ ❖ LATE SPRING to EARLY AUTUMN
H and S 25–38cm (10–15in)

Choose calibrachoas for hanging baskets, window boxes and containers, where their prolific and brightly coloured flowers will enchant you all summer long. Rather more elegant, but smaller in stature than the similar-looking petunias, these plants trail and spread, and associate well with most other annuals, including verbenas and helichrysum. Colours in this popular series include white, pink, yellow, orange, red and purple.

Dahlia 'Moonfire'
○ ❀ 🍂 ❖ MIDSUMMER to AUTUMN
H 90cm (3ft) S 60cm (24in)

With its dark bronze-purple leaves and pale yellow flowers, each with a soft-red centre, 'Moonfire' is perfect for adding late colour to borders. It will do well in containers, too, but dahlias need plenty of water, so make sure you can provide this. Other bedding dahlias include the Melody series and Gallery series, both with semi-double and double flowers, in a wide range of colours, and low-growing to 45cm (18in).

Diascia Wink series
○ ❄ ❖ SUMMER to AUTUMN
H and S 40cm (16in)

This diascia series comes in many colours, including white, oranges, pinks and reds, on upright plants that are perfect for containers or in a raised bed, gravel garden or border. They flower prolifically for months, especially if dead-headed regularly. They are sold as bedding, but the plants are perennial and although top-growth will be cut back by hard frosts, the crown should survive down to −8°C (18°F).

Helichrysum petiolare
○ ❋ pH ↑ ❖ SUMMER to AUTUMN
H and S 60–90cm (2–3ft)

Evergreen but frost-tender, this stiffly trailing shrub has attractive soft-hairy, grey leaves and makes excellent 'filling' for baskets and other planters, among both bright and pastel summer flowers. It bears off-white flowerheads in late summer, and these are good for drying. Good varieties include 'Limelight' (lime-green foliage, shown above) and 'Variegatum' (green leaves with white edges; H and S 30cm/12in).

Nemesia 'Amelie'
○ ❋ pH ↓ ❖ LATE SPRING to EARLY AUTUMN
H and S 30cm (12in)

Nemesias have abundant confetti-like flowers and are available in many shades. 'Amelie' is soft pink ageing to lilac, a colouring that is perfectly complemented by a light vanilla scent. It looks wonderful in pots on its own or perhaps with silver foliage plants. A frost-tender evergreen perennial, it can be overwintered indoors. 'Wisley Vanilla' is white with a more intense fragrance.

Pelargonium 'Vancouver Centennial'
○ ◑ ❋ pH ↑ ❖ SPRING to SUMMER
H 30cm (12in) S 20cm (8in)

Pelargoniums – popularly but incorrectly known as 'geraniums' – are great summer performers, with their bright flowers and often colourful foliage. If space is tight, this compact variety is particularly good value, with its clusters of star-shaped, bright scarlet flowers atop eye-catching jagged fresh green leaves, which are heavily splashed with dark red-brown. Dead-head regularly and overwinter indoors or propagate from cuttings.

Petunia Tumbelina series
○ ◑ ❋ 🍂 ❖ SUMMER to EARLY AUTUMN
H 25cm (10in) S 60cm (24in)

Showy, top-class trailing performers for baskets, planters and window boxes, Tumbelina petunias produce masses of scented, peony-like double blooms with ruffled petals. The range of shades has an 'antique' flavour, with a sumptuous choice of pinks and purples, some with heavy veining (such as 'Priscilla', shown above); there is also a pure white variety. Water the plants freely and dead-head regularly to ensure a continuous display.

Verbena Aztec series
○ ❋ ❖ SUMMER to AUTUMN
H 20cm (8in) S 45cm (18in)

Clusters of flowers in shades of red, purple, pink, coral and white are the obvious attraction of this group of verbenas. The vigorous, disease-resistant plants have been bred for a long flowering season (provided they are dead-headed regularly), together with good heat- and drought-tolerance. Grow in baskets and other containers, or as summer edging in beds and borders. The flowers attract bees and butterflies. Shown in the group above are 'Dark Red', 'Blue Velvet', 'Wild Rose', 'Coral'.

Viola Avalanche series
○ ◑ 🍂 ❖ SPRING to AUTUMN, WINTER
H and S to 23cm (9in)

There are many varied spring-, summer- and winter-flowering violas, and you may find this collection at any time of the year. Avalanche series violas have a slightly trailing habit and come in a range of traditional colours, including red, deep purple, lemon, cream and pink, some bicoloured. The lax habit makes it perfect for hanging baskets and other containers; it is ideal for the edge of a raised bed, too.

Index

Page numbers in *italics* refer to plants in the Recommended easy-care plants directory.

Acknowledgements

BBC Books and OutHouse would like to thank the following for their assistance in preparing this book: Andy McIndoe for advice and guidance; Robin Whitecross for picture research; Lesley Riley for proofreading; June Wilkins for the index.

Picture credits

Key t = top, b = bottom, l = left, r = right, c = centre

PHOTOGRAPHS

All photographs by Jonathan Buckley except those listed below.

David Austin Roses 62t, 77bc, br, tc & tr, 78

Ball Horticultural 90l & tc, 91tr

GAP Photos Matt Anker 14; Lee Avison 75tc; BBC Magazines Ltd 15b, 73bl; Pernilla Bergdahl 82tl; Richard Bloom 67tr, 69bc, 72br, 77l; Elke Borkowski 8, 12, 17, 30t; Nicola Browne 26; Carole Drake 82tc; Heather Edwards 4, 52b, 56b; Ron Evans 71tl; FhF Greenmedia 71bl; Suzie Gibbons 28; John Glover 50t, 68br, 71br, 91bl; Anne Green-Armytage 29; Jerry Harpur 69bl; Marcus Harpur 15t, 16; Charles Hawes 52t; Neil Holmes 69tr; Michael Howes 54t; Martin Hughes-Jones 67bc, 69tc, 70br & tr, 74tc, 76br, 76tc, 83bl, 90bc; Dianna Jazwinski 32; Geoff Kidd 70bc, 80tc; Fiona McLeod 20, 91br; Neil Overy 82br; Abby Rex 2/3; Howard Rice 81tr; Sabina Ruber 89cr; Trevor Sims 75tr; S&O 48b, 75bc; J S Sira 72tr, 75tl, 79tc; Lee Thomas 76tr; Maddie Thornhill 59; Visions 88bc; Jo Whitworth 50b, 66bl, 67tc, 69br; Rob Whitworth 25b; Don Wildridge 91tl; Steven Wooster 66bc, 67br, 67br; Dave Zubraski 71bc

Garden Picture Library/Getty Images Clive Nichols 13tr, 34; Michael Paul 31t

Garden World Images Tony Cooper 72tl

Sue Gordon 9, 75bl, 89br

Andrew McIndoe 65tl, bl & br, 66br & bl, 67tl & bl, 68l, bc & tc, 70bl, 71tc & tr, 72bc, 72tc, 73bc, br, tl, & tr, 74bl, bc & tr, 75br, 76bl, bc, & tl, 79bc & tr, 80bl & bc, 81l, br & tc, 82bc & tr, 83tc, 88l, tc & tr, 89bl, bc & tc, 90br & tr, 91bc & tc

Marianne Majerus Garden Images 70tc

Clive Nichols Garden Photography 10

Raymond Turner 30b

Bransford Webb Plant Company 68tr

Robin Whitecross 13tl, 18, 33, 56t, 81bc, 83tl

ILLUSTRATIONS

Caroline De Lane Lea 18, 47

Lizzie Harper 27, 29, 33, 39, 43

Sue Hillier 41

Janet Tanner 21, 46, 49, 51, 53, 55, 57

Thanks are also due to the following designers and owners whose gardens appear in the book:

Sue Andrews 12; Susan Berger 26; Justin Greer 15t; Iona Hilleary Landscape Design 20; Elaine Hughes 16; Christopher Masson 13tr, 34; Bob Parker, Wolverhampton, Staffordshire 60; Bob Purnell 15b; Sarah Raven, Perch Hill, East Sussex 35; Sue and Wol Staines, Glen Chantry, Essex 61; Joe Swift and Sam Joyce for The Plant Room 20; Sarah Taylor 50b; Alan Titchmarsh 25b; Gay Wilson, London 11; Helen Yemm, Ketley's, East Sussex 13b, 25, 58

While every effort has been made to trace and acknowledge all copyright holders, the publisher would like to apologize should there be any errors or omissions.